IN SEARCH OF JOHN

IN SEARCH OF JOHN

THE ABBEYLARA STORY OF DEPRESSION, LOSS AND A FAMILY'S QUEST FOR JUSTICE

Marie Carthy

HODDER
HEADLINE
IRELAND

First published in 2007 by Hodder Headline Ireland
A division of Hodder Headline

WRITTEN IN COLLABORATION WITH JUNE CONSIDINE

1

A CIP catalogue record for this title is available from the British Library.

ISBN 978 0 340 93645 0

Typeset in Sabon by Hodder Headline Ireland
Printed and bound in Great Britain by Clays Ltd, St Ives plc
Hodder Headline Ireland's policy is to use papers that are natural, renewable
and recyclable products and made from wood grown in sustainable forests.
The logging and manufacturing processes are expected to conform to the
environmental regulations of the country of origin.

The publishers would like to thank the Irish Examiner, The Irish Times *and
Keith Heneghan for their kind permission to use images in the book.*

Hodder Headline Ireland
8 Castlecourt Centre
Castleknock
Dublin 15, Ireland
A division of Hachette Livre UK Ltd.
338 Euston Road,
London NW1 3BH

www.hhireland.ie

Contents

In Search of John 11

Afterword by Sean Love 236

Acknowledgements 239

Appendix 1 244

To the memory of my beloved brother John,
and to all those who struggle with depression

Do not stand by my grave and weep,
I am not there I do not sleep.
I am a thousand winds that blow,
I am the diamond glints upon the snow,
I am the sunlight on ripened grain,
I am the gentle autumn rain,
I am the soft star that shines so bright
In Abbeylara late at night.

In loving memory of John Carthy
Whose life was taken tragically
On 20 April 2000, age twenty-seven years.

Prologue

Gardaí have sealed off the town of Abbeylara in County Longford after a man armed with a shotgun fired shots at them and then barricaded himself into a house. Some families have been moved from neighbouring houses for their safety. Gardaí have surrounded the house and made telephone contact with the man inside.
  – RTÉ report, 19 April 2000

This is how I will always remember it . . . that wet chilly evening, the wind blowing hard off the Atlantic. I cycled to work this morning but the weather turned during the day and now, as I lock up and make everything secure, I dread the long journey back to my apartment. I teach in the First Flight Crèche & Montessori School. It's a job I love, but a group of bright, lively children have taken their toll on my energy. When my employer, Linda, offers me a lift, I waste no time accepting it. I pack my bike into the boot of her jeep and climb inside. We leave the village of Furbo behind and head towards the seaside resort of Salthill, where I live.

Once inside my apartment, I set about preparing my evening meal. A cosy night stretches ahead of me, with nothing more strenuous to do than settling down with a plate of chicken curry and a few hours' relaxation in front of the television. It's a relief to kick off my shoes and draw the curtains against this blustery Galway night.

The rice is simmering on the hob when my mobile phone rings. I'm not expecting a call from anyone. It could be friends, Geraldine Heaney, perhaps, or Siobhan Judge, ringing to see if I want to catch a film or meet up for a drink. I enjoy socialising and have made many friends in the eight years since I moved from Longford to Galway. But not tonight, I think, as I pick up the phone.

My cousin, Ann Walsh, is on the other end of the line. Our mothers are sisters, close friends and neighbours, living only a few doors away from each other. Ann sounds subdued. I immediately know by her voice that something is seriously wrong at home.

'Things aren't good up here,' she confirms. 'John's locked himself into the house on his own and has his gun with him. The police have been called to talk him out.'

I try to take in the enormity of what she's telling me. Her words don't make any sense. I talked to John on the phone earlier. He was fine then, looking forward to the weekend, making plans. To add to my disbelief, Ann informs me that two guards from Salthill are coming to collect me in a squad car and bring me home to Abbeylara.

How? When? Why? I can only blurt out shocked questions, but the whys and wherefores don't really matter. John, my beloved brother, my only brother, is in trouble, and the police have been called to sort out the situation.

The apartment is silent after our phone call ends. Everything is as normal – the spicy smell of curry hanging in the air, the curtains blocking out the night, the television flickering without sound. Yet everything has changed utterly. I've no idea how long I'll be away. Nothing matters except reaching John as soon as possible. I immediately ring his mobile phone. No connection, just an operator's voice informing me that the caller is out of range and advising me to try again later.

I need someone with me for support, otherwise I'll start to panic, and that's not going to help anyone. I immediately think of Martin Shelly. He's known to his friends as Pepper and was one of the first people to befriend John when my brother moved to Galway a year ago. They worked together on a building site and remained friends even after John returned to Longford.

When Pepper answers his phone, I discover that Ann has already been in touch with him. She was unable to get a connection to my mobile number when she first tried to phone me and rang his house phone. He agreed to contact me and get me to ring her immediately. However, she successfully reached me when she tried my number again. He knows something is wrong, but not the details, and is equally disbelieving when I tell him what has occurred. He promises to be with me as soon as possible. He spoke to my mother, who seemed confident that the situation would be sorted out quickly. She has left her house and is staying with Ann's sister, Trisha Mahon, who lives a few miles away from Abbeylara.

Abbeylara, where I was reared, is a small rural village in County Longford. Ann's family, the Walshes, and my own family live on the outskirts of the village along a quiet stretch of the Toneymore Road. Nothing much ever happens there, apart from the normal activities of daily life. It's impossible to imagine the police outside our house – or John behind a window with a shotgun in his hand. The idea of a police car picking me up seems equally ludicrous, but Ann has made it clear I must return to Abbeylara as fast as possible.

We're a small family, just the two of us and my widowed mother, Rose.

John suffers from depression. For ten years I've seen the suffering it inflicts on him and admired the way he manages to control his illness. Being so close in age – only fourteen months separates us – we've always had a close and loving bond. We played together as children, socialised together when we grew older, enjoyed the same bands, shared the same friends. After I moved to Galway, we phoned each other on an almost daily basis, sometimes even ringing each other a few times during the day, especially when John was worried about something. I'd talked him through many difficult times and encouraged him to seek medical care when he needed it. We've seen each other through a lot over the years, but according to Ann, something has obviously gone wrong, and the need to be in Abbeylara overwhelms me.

As I pack some clothes and toiletries in my rucksack, I force myself to calm down, to remind myself that John would never harm himself, or anyone else. His shotgun is legally owned, used for shooting game. He's always treated his gun with respect, taking proper safety precautions, and would never turn it on himself, no matter how low he felt. My hands shake as I fasten the rucksack. I dread the journey, the miles we must cover before I can speak to him.

Pepper arrives a few minutes before the police and gives me a reassuring hug. Whatever is wrong with John will be sorted out as soon as we reach Abbeylara, he tells me, and I believe him. It's good to have him here with me. He's a big man, strong shoulders, solid and reliable in a crisis. A friend I can depend on. We'd planned to travel together to Abbeylara for the forthcoming Easter weekend. John had been looking forward to Pepper's first visit to our house and had been talking about the weekend when I phoned him at lunchtime. He'd wanted to introduce Pepper to his friends and show him around Abbeylara.

Shortly afterwards, a guard arrives from Salthill garda station. Seeing him standing there in his uniform, the seriousness of his expression, the situation seems even more frightening. I wonder what the residents will think as I'm escorted from the apartment block. What will the neighbours in Abbeylara think as I'm driven through the village in a squad car? Knowing how much Rose values her

14

privacy, I hope everyone will be indoors and the crisis sorted out as quietly as possible.

I confirm that I am Marie Carthy, and we follow the guard to an unmarked garda car where the driver is waiting. We settle ourselves into the back seat and head towards the open road. It's now nine o'clock. Only two hours have passed since I finished work, but the day is already fading into a distant memory. I keep asking the guards for information, but they claim to have no idea about what has occurred. It will probably take at least two hours to reach Abbeylara, and their only instructions are to ferry me there as fast as possible. I try John's mobile phone again, but the operator delivers the same message. Inwardly, I curse the network coverage to our house, which has always been poor. Apart from myself and Pepper talking to each other, there is silence in the car. The radio is switched off and the driver is driving at high speed. When my mobile phone rings, I answer it instantly, hoping it's John.

Patricia Leavey, a friend since my early schooldays, is ringing from Abbeylara to check if I'm okay. She tries to sound reassuring, but I can tell she's worried. She's waiting for me in a friend's house and will give me any help I need. I'm beginning to realise that what has happened to my brother is no longer a private domestic matter.

The squad car is going very fast. Saliva fills my mouth. I feel sick and am afraid I'll throw up. After we're on the road for over an hour, I ask the driver to stop somewhere so that I can use the bathroom. He drives into the car park of a hotel in Roscommon. I hurry with Pepper through the entrance, feeling dizzy as we step into the lights. People are eating, drinking, laughing together. They seem far away, seen through a haze as I hurry towards the Ladies. I can't get sick. Slowly, the dizziness and nausea pass.

At lunchtime, when I phoned John, I used the public phone across the road from the school and managed to reach him on his mobile. I look for a public phone in the hotel foyer and shove coins into the slot, trying once more to contact him. Again, I receive the same response. I'm beginning to hate the operator's monotone voice advising me to check again later.

The guards remain aloof, only speaking to me to ask directions. They must be aware of how worried I feel, but they conduct themselves through silence, doing their duty quickly and efficiently. I contact Patricia again. She's rung John twice in quick succession and managed to get through, but although he answered the phone, he didn't speak to her and kept hanging up. I don't understand why. John trusts her. On a number of occasions she visited him in hospital. He confided in her, told her how much he hated admitting himself to St Loman's Psychiatric Hospital in Mullingar when he could no longer handle his depression.

At Edgeworthstown, the driver asks for the fastest route to Abbeylara. He's driving at such speed he actually misses one of the turnings. About three miles from home, the other guard asks if I've any objections to the siren being used. I agree, hoping it will provide a clear passage through traffic. I'm beyond caring who sees or hears us. He rolls down the window and puts the siren on the roof. The whirring sound beats against my ears. Pepper grasps my hand, orders me to try and relax. I'll be no use to John if I lose my cool at this stage. Everything is going to be all right. I agree with him; contemplating anything else is too frightening. Space and time together, that's all we need to sort out whatever problems have affected John.

The first thing I notice as we enter the village is a satellite television van. It can't be possible – surely there isn't a television crew in Abbeylara reporting on John? Not only are the people of Abbeylara aware of what is happening at our house, but so, too, are the general public. Whatever John has done is making headlines, news bulletins. It'll be reported on television. If details of his plight have already been broadcast, he could be listening. He could have seen pictures on television. Many people close to him don't even realise he suffers from depression. I can't imagine him coming out of the house if he discovers all this attention is focused on him.

As we step out of the police car, I thank the guards from Galway for bringing me home. As arranged, Patricia and her sister, Ann, are waiting for us. We only have time for a brief conversation before Pepper and I are brought through a garda checkpoint and up the Toneymore Road, where more guards await our arrival. We're only allowed as far as my Aunty Nancy's house. This was where Rose went for advice when John became agitated. The house is empty now. The neighbours have also been evacuated. Only one house is occupied, illuminated by a sweeping spotlight. A megaphone is turned in its direction. Figures crouch behind the gatepost. Other uniformed guards stand nearby. Squad cards and jeeps are parked at the side of the road. The police have formed a complete cordon around the front and back of our house. This is worse than I dared imagine. It reminds me of a crime film, something I might have seen on television as I sat down to eat my evening meal.

My cousin Thomas Walsh comes over to greet me. We've been friends since childhood, have played in the fields surrounding our houses and treated each other's homes like our own. He drove straight from Cork as soon as his family contacted him and has already given details to the guards about John's medical history. Now the guards are anxious to interview me. As yet, these men are only faces. In time, their names will become familiar to me: Superintendent Joseph Shelly, who has overall responsibility for the so-called Abbeylara siege, and Superintendent Michael Byrne, the night scene commander.

My hopes that I'd be able to talk to John as soon as I arrived are quickly dashed. I'm to be interviewed by the guards before I make contact, and the interview will be conducted in Ballywillian, a small townland that runs along the back of our property. This is for safety reasons, I'm told. The guards don't want to drive past the house in case it attracts John's attention and he shoots at them. My sense of unreality grows as I step into the jeep with Thomas and Pepper. I simply can't understand how Rose's phone call to the local police could have created such a massive response. Thank God she's away from the scene. At least she's spared the sight of armed guards in flak jackets surrounding her home.

We're driven away by a uniformed guard. To reach Ballywillian along this route, we have to backtrack and drive through the town of Granard, which is about three miles outside Abbeylara. Traffic has been diverted away from Ballywillian and the road is eerily empty except for the guards. We're introduced to Detective Garda Michael Sullivan, who questions us on behalf of the negotiator, Detective Sergeant Michael Jackson. Both Detective Garda Sullivan and the negotiator are members of the Emergency Response Unit (ERU). I know little about the ERU, apart from the fact that they are an elite force trained to deal with highly charged criminal and terrorist situations. What on earth are they doing in Abbeylara? What is their connection to a quiet rural family who simply sought the assistance of the local force to calm a young man in the grip of a depressive episode?

I tell Garda Sullivan about John's illness and how it has affected his life. I also try to figure out the reasons why he's acting so out of character. Tomorrow is Holy Thursday. Ten years previously, our father died on a Holy Thursday. By a strange coincidence, Rose's father also died on another Holy Thursday and, although the feast of Easter falls on a different date each year, Easter week is always a particularly poignant time for my family. Then there's the question of our old house, which will soon be demolished. A new house is being built beside it and, by order of the County Council, the old house must be razed to the ground as soon as the building work is complete. John is feeling the pressure of the move, trying to get everything organised on time for Rose. This sense of responsibility has become heightened as the date of the move draws nearer.

This is only one of a number of things that have been weighing heavily on his mind in recent months. He lived for almost a year in Galway, but in February he was dismissed from a building project where he worked as a plasterer. He believed this was an unfair dismissal, and despite the situation being eventually sorted out to everyone's satisfaction, the experience upset him deeply. Around the same time, his relationship with his girlfriend came to an end, and he blamed himself for its acrimonious ending. As I discuss this with Detective Garda Sullivan, I ask him not to mention the relationship in case it upsets John any further. Finally, there is the question of the gardaí. Such a strong and obvious presence will do nothing to defuse the situation, especially as John doesn't trust some of the local guards.

'Just leave him alone,' I plead. 'The main thing you shouldn't do is confront him. Give him space and he'll come out of his own accord.'

Pepper agrees with me and also gives the ERU officer any information about John that he believes will be useful. I look towards the back of my house. It's too dark to make out the details, and I can only imagine John inside, terrified and hostile, lost in some dark space in his mind. Garda Sullivan promises to arrange contact for me with John – but not yet. He's adamant about this. Nor will we be allowed near the house. I know by the tone of his voice that the situation is out of my hands. We continue to hang around, hoping things will change and we'll be driven back up to the Toneymore Road.

The trees are only now beginning to bud and loom darkly above the jeep. It's bitterly cold. I can't stop shaking. Why have I been driven home at such high speed in a garda car, only to be left on the sidelines, unable to do anything to ease the situation? Eventually, when there's no sign of any effort being made to enable contact with John, we're driven back to the village. Branches flash past the windows and the quiet waters of Lake Killana, where we'd fished together as children, lap silently against the pebble shore.

The Devine family lives in the centre of Abbeylara village. Ronan, their son, has been friends with John since they were in primary school together. I'm welcomed into their house after returning from my interview with Detective Garda Sullivan. The driver promises to come back and pick us up as soon as the arrangements for contact are put in place. He's told by Mr Devine that a key will be left in the front door. The gardaí can enter the house and let us know immediately if we're needed at the scene. We wait for his return. Midnight comes and goes. Again, I try and fail to make contact with John's phone. I wonder if he's switching it on and off to avoid speaking to the guards? I also phone my mother, Rose. Her distress is obvious, but it's impossible to go to her under the circumstances. I know her niece Trisha and her sister Nancy will support and comfort her as best they can. I need to be close to the Toneymore Road when the call comes to speak to John.

Another hour passes, then another. A new day has begun. My life has changed unimaginably from what it was a mere twelve hours ago. Many lives will be changed by the events being played out in Abbeylara, but none of us can possibly envisage the tragic consequences that will unfold over the following hours. My heart is filled with love and trepidation for my brother as I await the garda driver's return. He never shows up. I struggle constantly to keep my panic under control. John must be cold, hungry, terrified by what his actions have unleashed. Is he pacing the floor or huddled under the window? Is he thinking of me, wondering where I am? Have the guards told him I'm here, just down the road in the village, waiting for an opportunity to speak to him? I'm surrounded by friends, yet I feel so alone. But my loneliness is nothing compared to how he must be feeling as he hides in the shadows of the house where we shared the carefree years of our childhood.

Chapter One

In the parish of Abbeylara there are two well-preserved remains of stone circles. There are also in this area surviving traces of what appear to be megalithic burials. There is no doubt of the antiquity of these stone circles and of their importance as archaeological remains of the Bronze Age period of our history. They stand as memorials to those who recognised the sun as the centre of the universe, the source of all life.
  – From the County Longford Heritage/Historical website

The photograph is yellow and a bit dog-eared with age. In it, a young woman stands beside a motorcycle, a BSA 175 model. I saw the photograph for the first time when I began to write this book and encouraged my mother to talk to me about her young days in Abbeylara. This was her motorcycle. She enjoyed the thrill of the open road, the freedom it gave her when she wasn't working on the family farm. She also loved dancing. It was the era of the big show bands: Larry Cunningham, Big Tom & the Mainliners, The Drifters, and all the other popular showbands who regularly played the Eldorado in Oldcastle or the Granada Ballroom in Granard. Rose was equally light-footed when it came to céilí dancing and, as

21

Abbeylara is situated on a crossroads, many céilí bands played under the stars while the young and the not-so-young danced the night away.

For all her gaiety, Rose Donohue was introduced to tragedy early in life when her mother injured her back in an accident and was confined to a wheelchair. She died when Rose was only six years old. Her father's family were mill owners in Killasona, a small townland about two miles outside Abbeylara. This was where Rose spent her early years but, after her mother's death, Owen Donohue moved his young family – a son, Patsy, and his two daughters, Nancy and Rose – to a farm in Toneymore. Rose was his youngest child and, like her brother and sister, her days were busy on the farm. She worked the bog, fed the livestock and gathered the eggs. It was a hard-working, simple way of life carried out in an era when farms were loud with the cackle of hens and turkeys and the pigsty was as familiar as the cow byre and the stable. Owen supplemented his farm income by doing occasional work with Bord na Móna, which was the biggest employer in that boggy area of the Irish midlands.

My own father, John Carthy, a local man from Abbeylara, also worked for Bord na Móna throughout his working life. He was a fitter in their Coolnagun plant in north Westmeath. Before cars became a regular feature in the village, a lorry collected the local men to bring them to work in the mornings and home again in the evenings.

The village of Abbeylara has changed only a little since then. St Bernard's Church still remains a focal point, with the small school John and I attended close beside it. There's a shop and two pubs, but the post office, like many such institutions in rural Ireland, no longer exists. The ruins of the historical monastery that gave Abbeylara its name (Mainister Leathratha – abbey of the half rath or little rath) is still a familiar landmark on the approach to the village. Today, all that remains of this once-famous Cistercian monastery are the central tower and some adjacent walls. Recently, there's been a flourish of development in the village, with new houses seeming to mushroom overnight, but Abbeylara remains a small, close-knit community.

After my parents married, Rose moved into the Carthy family home that had belonged to her husband's father. When John was born, her motorcycle was exchanged for a pram. Only that single photograph provides a clue to the adventurous personality of a young woman whom I would always know as my sensible, hard-working mother.

John was born in Mullingar General Hospital on 9 October 1972, a dark-haired baby with deep green eyes. According to Rose, he had a contented, easy-going nature. Fourteen months later, when I was born in Holles Street Hospital in Dublin and carried back to Abbeylara to make his acquaintance, he accepted me into his life without complaint or any signs of sibling jealousy. He would do anything for me as I struggled to my feet and began to toddle after him. He was my whole world, my only friend.

We were quite young when Nancy, my mother's sister, moved from Dublin back to Abbeylara and settled into a bungalow just a few doors away from us. Suddenly, much to our delight, we had an extended family of five cousins: Maura, Ann, Rosaleen, Trisha and Thomas. The Walsh family quickly adjusted to their new surroundings. Thomas was around our own age and lost no time joining in our games and roaming the fields with us.

John and I started school on the same day. We walked hand in hand from our house to the small one-storey building. We didn't know any of the other children who were also starting on the same day. Some of them were crying as they were ushered into their new classroom, and Rose, whose life had been busy with the demands of two mischievous children, also shed a few tears as she said goodbye to us. But we were laughing as we settled side by side into our desk, no nerves, just anticipation and excitement. In those days, I was very dependent on John. Fourteen months is a big age gap to a small child, and he remained my hero – lively, friendly, outgoing. I was the quiet one, shy and awkward in company, only feeling secure when he was beside me.

We sat together during that first year. As we were preparing to move into Senior Infants, our teacher decided that John had made sufficient progress to go directly into First Class. Being part of a small school meant that he simply moved to another area in the same classroom, yet I saw this as a separation and wept with fear at the thought of it. However, it forced me to come out of myself, and I began to make my own friends, just as John was doing. A year later, when he moved into a different classroom, I waved him goodbye and got on with my own school life.

Our childhood was similar to that of many other children living in quiet rural communities. Boredom and isolation could have tempted us to devilment, but we made our own fun and took the wide open spaces around us for granted. We climbed trees, played hide-and-seek and chased each other in the surrounding fields. A 'money tree' grew in our garden. For some reason we picked this tree out for special attention, and when the golden leaves fell to the ground, we collected them and buried them in heaps under the clay, hoping, perhaps, that they would turn to crocks of gold.

We had forests with shadowy trails of spruce, larch, oak and ash to explore. Nearby, Lough Killana and Lough Derragh were adventurous places to paddle and fish when we grew older. Uncle Patsy had inherited his father's farm and it was only 200 metres from our home. He never married and treated us as his own children, just as our Aunty Nancy did. The village also had its challenges, especially the old monastery ruins, with its crumbling walls. It was founded in 1211 by the Anglo-Norman lord, Richard de Tuit, and I often wondered if the echo of our voices raised the ghosts of the past. One Halloween evening, I climbed the steps to the summit, egged on by my friends, knowing I was breaking rules and that my mother would be horrified if she found out. From the top there was a magnificent view over the countryside and a wind that almost toppled me over the edge. In years to come, I would discover that Rose, too, had disobeyed her father and made the same perilous journey up the ancient steps.

I smoked my first cigarette at the tender age of six. John, aged seven, was equally inexperienced when we both lit up. It was summer time, a hot, drowsy day, and we were bored at home. Dad was at work, and Rose, who wasn't feeling well, had gone to bed for a rest, believing we could be trusted to behave ourselves for a few hours. We found her packet of Carroll's cigarettes and decided to experiment. Both my parents smoked, and it looked so simple. We hid in the spare room and blew thick bellows of smoke up the chimney of an open hearth fireplace. We felt grown up and sophisticated until Trisha, my cousin and godmother, entered the house, followed our trail of smoke and caught us in the act. Amazingly, we weren't violently ill, even though we'd smoked almost an entire packet of ten. It's ironic to think of the significance cigarettes would have for John many years later but, fortunately, on that sunny day, we'd little idea of what lay ahead for both of us.

John received his First Holy Communion in 1980. Preparations for the big day began early that year. I remember how nervous he was about the 'sins' he would have to confess and how seriously he rehearsed their telling. It all seemed very mysterious and exciting. We could commit as many sins as we liked and still be forgiven once we entered the confession box and whispered them into the ears of the priest. I can still picture him dressed in his navy blue suit on that special day as our former parish priest, Fr Michael Egan, placed the host on his tongue. He looked so vulnerable and innocent, so open to the belief that he was receiving the body of Jesus Christ into his soul.

Growing up, we remained inseparable. The deep bonds we had shared as small children showed no signs of loosening. Fishing, handball, cycling, football and tennis were just some of the activities that filled our days. We watched our favourite television programmes

– *Wanderly Wagon*, *Blue Peter* and, later, *Grange Hill*, *Chips*, *Neighbours* and, John's favourite, the wrestling matches. Like any brother and sister, we had our disagreements but, thankfully, they never lasted long.

The high point of our summers was an annual trip to the Steam Engine Rally in Stradbally, Co. Laois. It was an opportunity for my father to meet up with friends who, like himself, were fascinated by the operational models on display and to hunker in front of strange noisy contraptions that throbbed with a fast mechanical beat. I remember the old-fashioned steam engines with their high red wheels and hissing steam, the sheep-dog demonstrations, the microlight planes and classic cars, the motor bikes and the amusement arcade that drew us like a magnet with its flashing lights and jingle of coins. Our favourite activities were watching the hot-air-balloon show and riding the narrow gauge railway.

The next big stepping stone for John was his Confirmation, which took place in 1985. This was yet another important moment in his journey towards adulthood, and there were even more in-depth preparations for the receiving of this sacrament. He took Patrick as his Confirmation name, after Uncle Patsy, and Jerry Flynn, my cousin Maura's husband, was his sponsor. John was their regular babysitter, and their children looked forward to the nights when he was left in charge. The house was always quiet and the family fast asleep when Maura and Jerry returned home from their nights out. On this occasion, Jerry escorted him to the altar, where he placed his hand on John's shoulder and promised to put the 'Gifts of the Spirit' into practice.

As the years flew by, we had only one big worry: our father's failing health. Dad was a hard-working man who enjoyed growing his own vegetables, saving turf on the bog and gathering the hay during summer. Politics and current affairs interested him. When he had time to spare, he would be found reading the newspaper or a current-affairs magazine. He was keen to keep abreast with what was happening outside our small community, yet he was also involved in the heart of village life.

As a young man, he had developed bronchitis. He often told me about the times he worked the bogs in all kinds of rough weather. On one occasion, he took a lift home on top of a hay lorry. It began to lash rain and he was drenched to the skin when he finally reached his destination; he developed pneumonia. This left him with chronic bronchitis, which became an increasingly difficult complaint to control as he grew older.

Like John would later become, Dad was a chain smoker who tried many times to quit. All his attempts failed. He was well and truly addicted to nicotine. As his health worsened, I often lay awake at night worried that he was going to die. To lose anyone from my family seemed like a far-off nightmare, yet listening to him coughing in the small hours, the nightmare seemed a little closer. His health further deteriorated when he developed heart disease and was hospitalised on a number of occasions. In time, even walking was a problem, and he had an oxygen container by his bedside. When the local doctor told us that he was 'living on borrowed time', I was too young to understand what he meant. Had I realised that Dad's time with us was 'borrowed' from death, I would have been heartbroken. Fortunately, the meaning escaped me, and I was able to convince myself he would recover.

Every Saturday, John helped out on Patsy's farm. He was driving Patsy's tractor from the age of eleven and doing a man's work around the farm. His early experiment with smoking and the ticking off that followed were forgotten once he became a teenager. He started smoking in his early teens and often shared a packet of cigarettes with Thomas at the back of a haystack. Thankfully, they never burned Patsy's farm down, and our uncle probably turned a blind eye to their furtive activities.

John's secondary education began in 1985 when he attended Ardscoil Phadraig in Granard. His friends nicknamed him 'Smirky' because he was always smiling. His happy-go-lucky personality helped him make friends easily. Cnoc Mhuire and Ardscoil Phadraig are the two secondary schools in Granard. I chose Ardscoil Phadraig to be with John and followed him a year later. I was a diligent student and enjoyed my subjects, especially the much-derided Irish classes, which were my favourite.

John was an average football player and usually played as a half forward when chosen for his team. He also enjoyed hurling, but his favourite competitive sport was handball, where he was considered to be a skilled competitor. It never mattered which sport he played, though – what was important to John was the challenge of competing, the team camaraderie, the thrill of winning. His trophies were always proudly displayed at home. I also loved playing hurling and wanted to compete alongside the boys. John didn't approve of this ambition, especially when, much to his mortification, I was once chosen to play in goal for one of their matches.

Ronan Devine, one of John's closest friends, lived in the house opposite St Bernard's Church. His family always made John welcome when he went to their house to play pool. He was an excellent player and frequently won on the break. When we played pool together, I found it hard to get a shot if he had the break. It could be very frustrating to play against him, yet also great fun as he joked his way through each frame.

As soon as he was old enough to legally hold a licence, he began driving my father's red Fiat 127. One afternoon, I accompanied him in the car to Patsy's farm. A schoolfriend, Regina Masterson, came to keep me company. After John started helping Patsy around the farm, I managed to get the keys and decided to experiment. John had made driving look so effortless. With Regina strapped into the passenger seat, I turned the ignition. John heard the engine roaring and came running into view just as I was driving down the laneway towards the main road. In the rear-view mirror I watched him chasing after the car, yelling at us to stop, his running hampered by his Wellington boots. All we could do was laugh, but our laughter was soon silenced as I stamped on the pedals and tried to bring the car to a halt. Needless to say, John was far from amused when he caught up with us and ordered us out. Behind his fury there was the very real fear that we would have injured ourselves, or worse. He was my big brother, always looking out for me. It was a long time before I was allowed behind the wheel of a car again.

When tragedy struck our young lives for the first time, it wasn't my father we mourned, but Patsy, our beloved uncle. He'd also worked with Bord na Móna and, on the day he died, had been feeling unwell. On his way home from work, he called in to Nancy. Just as he was about to sit down for a cup of tea, he suffered a massive heart attack and died on the spot. It was a balmy day, perfect for hay-making, and we were turning the hay at home when a neighbour hurried down the road to tell Rose the tragic news. We couldn't believe that someone who had seemed so healthy could go from us so suddenly. John, who had spent so many hours working with him on the farm, missed him sorely. For all of us, it was difficult coming to terms with death and my worries about my father's health increased.

After Patsy passed away, John inherited his Ferguson 20 tractor. It was parked at our family home, and John would occasionally use it for carrying out various chores. One afternoon, he drove it down the driveway to collect turf from the bog. The tractor went out of control, and he crashed straight through our next-door neighbour's wooden fence and onto their freshly cut lawn. Luckily, our neighbours were away on that day, but I can still see the look of horror on John's face as he sat on the tractor in the middle of their churned-up lawn. As soon as I realised he was unharmed, all I could do was laugh. Fortunately, our neighbours also had a sense of humour and were fine about the damage when they came home. Over the following days, John erected and painted a new fence, and the incident did nothing to dampen his love of driving.

Our father's health continued to worsen. For the last eighteen months of his life, he was often admitted to hospital, sometimes for up to two weeks at a time. John took us to visit him every day. I found it extremely upsetting, seeing my father so helpless and ill. No matter how much I tried to deny it, I had to accept that he would not be with us much longer.

On one particular evening, I decided to stay at home with Regina and watch a video. I was opting out, a teenager unable to cope with her father's unbearable pain. Later that evening, John arrived home, upset and freezing cold. When he was driving Rose to the hospital, a horse jumped out in front of Dad's car and plunged its hooves through the windscreen, shattering the glass. John was unhurt, but Rose had to go to hospital to receive stitches and would later suffer from post-traumatic stress. The gardaí were contacted, but the horse fled before they arrived. Its rightful owner was never found.

Not wanting to put unnecessary stress on our father when he was so ill, John never told him what happened. He knew that Dad would have wanted the car brought home, so he drove it back to Abbeylara with no windscreen to protect him from the cold and had it repaired the following day. Even at such a young age, he looked after us at all times.

He was seventeen when Dad passed away on 12 April 1990. We had been expecting him to die but kept holding on to the belief that, somehow, by our sheer willpower and his love for us, he would live a while longer. On the day he died, we'd gone shopping in Mullingar before visiting the hospital. It was Easter week and, as well as the usual grocery shopping, we had to buy Easter eggs for ourselves and our extended family. We completed our shopping and went to the hospital. Dad seemed to be asleep, his skin warm and soft to touch. I shook his arm, called his name, told him we were there at his bedside.

For once, I wasn't conscious of his laboured breathing. Instead, I heard only a peaceful silence. As I bent over him, I realised he wasn't breathing at all. It seemed as if he had simply dozed off while waiting for us to arrive. The nurses came when we called them and stared at him in disbelief.

'He was in great form all morning,' they told us. 'He had his usual shave and was walking around the ward for a while. Then he went back to bed for a rest.'

Death had crept gently upon him. Eighteen months of intense suffering had come to an end. We tried to take comfort from the peaceful expression on his face, but standing by his bedside, his hand still warm in mine, the stiffness of death not yet on his face, our future seemed bleak and empty without him.

Over the next few days, a constant flow of sympathisers came to our house to pay their respects. In such a small community as Abbeylara, no one is ever alone, and the death of a neighbour draws people together in an effort to help the bereaved family in practical ways. John travelled in the hearse on the evening of our father's removal to the parish church. The hearse and mourners paused for an instant outside our family home to allow Dad to bid us all a last farewell.

His funeral mass was held on Easter Sunday morning. Our secondary-school chaplain sang the gospel reading, and as I stared at my father's coffin, I was overcome with grief at how much I'd lost. I'd never see him again, hear his footsteps, his voice calling my name. I kept thinking about places we'd visited, how he'd always called me 'Daddy's girl', the doll he'd bought me for one of my birthdays, our yearly outings to the Steam Rally – all the little events and the big occasions, all the space he'd filled in our lives shut off for ever.

Throughout the following weeks, we got by with the help of our relations, friends and neighbours. But John was our greatest support through those dark, lonely days. He was the 'man of the house' now, and, although he was studying for his Leaving Certificate, he believed he needed to be there for my mother and myself.

Unfortunately, he contracted chicken pox during his Leaving Certificate and had to be isolated in a room to sit the exams. His self-determination and dedication helped him through each day. He was pleased with the results he achieved, and they enabled him to accept a place in Warrenstown Horticultural College, Co. Meath.

He bought his own car, an Opel Cadet, when he was seventeen. I remember him driving it home, the sun glinting off the green metallic sheen when we went outside to inspect it. It was his cherished possession and was maintained in peak condition. The big craze at that time was the CB radio. John had one installed in his car, as did a couple of his friends. He spent many hours talking to friends and making new ones. I often joined him and loved listening to the craic over the airwaves.

Like my mother before him, dancing was another interest. At the time, the local hotspot was a disco in Cavan. Transport there and back was organised with a local bus travelling from Granard every Saturday night and dropping those who lived in Abbeylara back to the village after it was over. When John attended his first disco, I was annoyed at being unable to go with him. To me, fourteen months meant nothing, but to my mother, it was everything. I was forced to watch from the sidelines as he got ready for his big night out. However, being John, I didn't have to wait for long. Within a short time he'd talked Rose into allowing me to go dancing with him at the Carrick Springs, Blazers and Fountain Blue nightclubs on the occasional Friday or Saturday night. Like most young people starting out in life, we knew how to enjoy ourselves. As our circle of friends widened, John began going out with girls. He was particularly keen on one girl, and their relationship was to last for about a year.

John began his horticulture course in 1991. Over a number of summers, he'd been employed in the local garden centre and had also worked with a landscaper from Longford. It was our first time apart. Without him or my father, the house seemed unnaturally quiet. Slowly, Rose and I began to adjust to our new situation. Every weekend, John returned home from Warrenstown College to ensure we had everything we needed. His sense of duty was strong but, in retrospect, it must have been a huge responsibility for any young man to carry.

I attended my debs in my final year in secondary school. I'd looked forward to this special night for ages and enjoyed discussing all the aspects of this important occasion with my friends. I was delighted to discover that a girl in my class had invited John to be her partner, which meant we could attend the debs together. Although John saw himself as a man of the world, he was as shy as most young men when it came to such formal occasions and was acutely embarrassed purchasing an orchid for her.

Before the big night arrived, fate seemed determined to single me out for punishments that should never be inflicted on any aspiring debutante. I had an accident playing football and was on crutches. To make matters worse, I used a fake tan lotion to achieve an all-over tan and came out in an all-over rash instead. While I was still trying to deal with the horror of this discovery, John went into Granard and bought me a special cream to try and ease the itch. The only way to cover my arms was to wear a pair of long gloves up to my elbows. I had to keep them on even when I was eating the meal. I still remember him laughing across the table at me as I tried to manage my knife and fork and keep my gloves away from the gravy.

We were happy to see John pursuing his career in horticulture. Our father had loved his garden, and John was showing the same green-fingered skills. Yet it was during those early months in college that he began to display the first signs of depression. Initially, such signs were easy to explain away. His moods fluctuated, but why not? He was studying hard, then coming home at weekends to look after the chores my father would normally have undertaken. His grief was still raw and unresolved, so it was easy to explain his sleeplessness, the need to talk incessantly, his sudden irritabilities. Excuses could always be found to account for his elation, which could sweep him along on its crest, then just as suddenly leave him dejected and withdrawn. I was aware that everyone, including myself, had ups and downs. Our father had only died two years previously. Happiness, sadness, even anger were normal emotions, an essential part of daily life. Or so I tried to convince myself. But a time came when we could no longer ignore the ever-increasing evidence that all was not well with John.

Along with his elation, his alternating down periods meant that he had very little energy. He told me he felt worthless and was unable to lift himself from this sense of hopelessness. He lost interest in his studies and his usual sporting activities. His self-esteem plummeted and was combined with guilt over our father's death. Despite all our reassurances to the contrary, he believed he was letting our father down, especially as his depression meant he had to miss his Christmas examinations. When he returned to college in January, he felt under pressure to make up for lost time, which added to his stress. It was difficult to watch my outgoing, friendly brother becoming ground down under the weight of real or imagined worries.

His first decision to manage his illness was made when he agreed to contact our family doctor. Dr Cullen arrived to our house shortly after we phoned him. Before, he had always attended us for minor ailments and the usual childhood illnesses. This was different. John agreed to admit himself to St Loman's Hospital in February 1992 as a voluntary in-patient. He was diagnosed as suffering from endogenous depressive illness and prescribed Gamanil and Xanax oral medication. Suddenly, we were looking into a deep, frightening well – and we had no knowledge of what lay beyond the dark surface.

Chapter Two

Bipolar affective disorder is a mood disorder that affects approximately 1% of the population. It was previously called manic depression. It affects both men and women equally and is not related to socio-economic status. The disorder is generally characterised by episodes of elation and depression with a normal mood in between. The first episode is usually before the age of thirty. The elation may be described as hypomania or mania depending on the severity of the mood disturbance, with mania being a more severe form of hypomania.

– Barr Tribunal report, Chapter 3: Bipolar Affective Disorder, Its Nature, Diagnosis and Treatment

A small community bonds together in times of trouble, but there's still a stigma attached to depression that's never applied to physical illness. John was aware of this stigma, and so he tried to hide his depression, especially when, during one of his voluntary admissions to hospital, he was diagnosed as suffering from a bipolar disorder. This didn't mean he was weak or unstable, yet some people didn't understand the nature of this illness and gave him a difficult time about his hospitalisation. Remarks such as 'Pull yourself together' and 'Can't you see what effect this is having on your family?' only added to his pressure and did nothing to help the situation.

According to statistics from Aware, the voluntary organisation established to assist people affected by depression, over 300,000 people in Ireland experience depressive illness at any one time. Estimates also suggest that approximately one in fourteen workers is affected. Bipolar disorder normally begins in adolescence or, as in John's case, in early adulthood. It can also occur when a person is in their forties and fifties and may persist for life. There is no cure yet; it is only controlled through the right medication and attitude. John read numerous books on depression in a bid to understand his illness, and, over a period of years, he voluntary admitted himself on four occasions to St Loman's Hospital. He was unhappy there and, at his own request, was referred to Dr Shanley, a consultant psychiatrist in St Patrick's Hospital, Dublin.

The successful management of his illness involved taking medication each day and regularly visiting his doctor. Because of the travelling distances involved between Abbeylara and Dublin, it was arranged that John's lithium levels would be monitored by Dr Cullen. As a result, monthly blood tests were carried out on him to check that he was within the therapeutic range.

Episodes of bipolar disorder may last for weeks or months. This can cause much distress to the sufferer's family and friends. For our family, it was a steep and difficult learning curve, but John's awareness of his symptoms helped us cope. In an earlier medical diagnosis, our father's death was considered to be a significant factor in the onset of his bipolar disorder. It was claimed that he had never dealt properly with his grief, yet to all outward appearances, John was like any other normal young man growing into adulthood and moving on with his life. He still retained his affable personality, his mischievous sense of humour, enjoyed having a few pints with friends, played pool and handball. He trusted Dr Shanley and had great faith in his ability to help him through the difficult times. When I could, I'd accompany him to the hospital or book his appointments at St Patrick's out-patients' department. Just as he had looked out for me throughout our childhood and after our father's death, I now took over that role and was willing to help in any way I could.

I moved to Galway in 1992 after successfully completing my Leaving Certificate. At first I studied hotel and catering in the regional training college but changed my mind and applied for a course in the Montessori method of teaching. I loved Galway, the people, the wonderful scenery, the buzz of the city with its arts and music and sense of its historic past. As part of a work experience, I spent two months in Belgium, which gave me a chance to visit Bruge, Brussels, Antwerp and Paris on my weekends off.

After graduating, I decided to settle in Galway. For a time, I worked as a classroom assistant in a primary school and gained experience in every age group from pre-school to sixth class. John visited me regularly. I was relieved to see that he, too, was coping well with life in Abbeylara. The years that passed were uneventful, apart from his involvement in two accidents. The first occurred in 1993, when he was loading a trolley with bread when he worked in the Pat the Baker Bakery in Granard. When he became trapped between two trolleys, he suffered an injury to his back and another to his left side. The injuries that occurred were physical, but the accident was a shock to his nervous system and, four months later, he admitted himself for treatment to St Loman's Hospital. It was becoming obvious to us that the frail line John walked between depression and elation could easily be upset by any traumatic event. Afterwards, he decided he'd like to work in the construction industry and took up plastering as his trade.

I remained his closest confidante. I soon learned to recognise the signs that his mood was changing: his rapid, intense speech, his elation or his anxieties which were out of proportion to the reality of particular situations. He regularly attended Aware meetings and often asked me to accompany him. Gradually, I, too, began to understand the nature of the disorder. The self-help group was extremely supportive, and we also attended lectures on depression given by Dr McKeon. As Director of the Mood Disorder Treatment Programme and the Depression Research Unit in St Patrick's, he has written many informative articles on depression, and John read them avidly.

Unfortunately, in February 1997, he was involved in a car accident in the early hours of a Sunday morning. He injured his right arm, which left him with a small scar and diminished power in his hand and arm. This often affected him when he was working, but I was more concerned about the psychological effects, remembering how distressed and agitated he had been when he suffered the work-related accident four years previously. He had been in perfect health before his car accident, but afterwards he had difficulty sleeping and was extremely nervous about travelling in cars. Dr Cullen continued to see him throughout March and April. When he visited Dr Shanley in May, his psychiatrist noted that the crash had been a 'very significant' event in John's life and that the stress symptoms were psychological rather than a manifestation of his illness. Sleeping tablets were prescribed, and he continued to have blood tests to monitor his condition, which showed the same therapeutic results as they had done prior to his accident and were without any signs of side effects. Dr Shanley believed his problems were suggestive of post-traumatic stress rather than an episode of bipolar disorder. John recovered from his accident, but unbeknownst to him, his life was changing in ways he could never have foreseen.

After Patsy died, John inherited his shotgun. He became a member of the local gun club and enjoyed shooting game as well as clay-pigeon shooting. As a result of the skills he acquired as a plasterer, he was able to assist with the rebuilding of the old Abbeylara handball alley. Over the years, the handball alley had become quite run down and was in danger of being demolished. It was the only sports-designated area in Abbeylara for young people, and the community was strongly opposed to its demolition. Between 1997 and 1998, a number of the locals, including John, decided to refurbish the alley, taking on the project on a voluntary basis. It was hard work but lots of fun, and John felt great pride in being part of this communal effort.

However, a rumour began to circulate shortly afterwards. No one was ever able to say who started it, but because John's history of depression was known in his community, it didn't take long to spread. It was alleged that he was annoyed by the presence of children in the handball alley who prevented him finding a slot to play. The rumour was that he'd threatened to shoot them if they didn't clear off. At the time, John knew nothing about this accusation. He continued with his normal sporting activities in both the handball alley and the gun club.

John had been working for a local businessman, but they had parted company after a disagreement. This difference of opinion soon became local knowledge. The wife of John's ex-employer mentioned the rumour circulating around Abbeylara to two of the local guards in Granard garda station. She believed it was wrong that someone with John's medical history should have access to a shotgun and feared that the dispute might cause him to harm her husband and her family. This was an informal conversation and was never lodged as an official complaint. The woman in question would later admit that the allegation was third-hand. Her husband also admitted he'd never been threatened by John, nor had any of her children ever heard him make such a comment in the handball alley. Yet, despite such flimsy evidence, the guards decided to take this woman's worries seriously and to confiscate John's legally licensed shotgun. How they went about this still fills me with anger. I was in Galway when it was decided and, like John, had no idea that such an action could come about on the basis of local gossip and rumour.

John was informed by one of the local guards that a direction had been issued by a higher authority that all licensed guns in the area were to be taken into custody for inspection. He handed over his gun as requested. This was August 1998, and he had no reason to suspect that this explanation was a lie. The gardaí in Granard believed that if they disclosed to him the true reason for confiscating his gun, he could have refused to voluntarily hand it over. They obviously never considered discussing the accusation with him and checking out whether or not he had made such threats. It was easier to act on misinformation, and, in doing so, I believe my brother was wronged twice over: once by a false allegation and then by the gardaí's assumption that because he suffered from episodic depressions, he was incapable of dealing with the truth.

Chapter Three

Ultimately, it emerged that the only possible justification for taking the gun was that Mr Carthy had previously suffered from mental illness and that step was taken without seeking any medical information or opinion to justify it. An important consequence of the garda conduct is that the creation of one cause for Mr Carthy's distrust of and antagonism towards the gardaí (which loomed large at Abbeylara) would not have arisen. That might have improved the possibility of successful negotiation with him.

    – Barr Tribunal report, Chapter 8: Conclusions

Over the next few months, John called to Granard garda station on a number of occasions looking for the return of his gun. Unable to understand why it was only his gun that had been confiscated, he demanded an explanation. On 6 October 1998, the guards were no longer able to keep the truth from him. At a meeting with Superintendent Cullinane, the real reason was finally revealed. John phoned me that night, shocked and disgusted by what he'd been told. He was also deeply offended that such vicious stories had been circulating behind his back. Superintendent Cullinane, who has since retired, told John his gun would only be returned on the recommendation of his doctor.

John approached Dr Cullen and asked for a letter of support. Still smarting from the lies he'd been told and the way he'd been fobbed off every time he called to the police station, he admitted during his consultation with his doctor that he would never again voluntarily hand over his gun to the guards. Dr Cullen could see he was deeply upset and decided to postpone his decision to write such a letter until he saw how John settled down.

At his next meeting with his psychiatrist in Dublin, John asked Dr Shanley to help him retrieve his gun. Seeing that he was in good health and showing no symptoms of his illness, Dr Shanley agreed to write the letter. John, ashamed to admit that people who knew him well had circulated such stories behind his back, never mentioned the real reason his gun had been taken.

Dr Shanley's letter was forwarded to the guards in Granard. John completed his application for a firearms certificate, and Rose also wrote a letter of consent, allowing the gun to be kept, as it always had been, in our family home. His shotgun was eventually returned four months after it had been confiscated. There were no further complaints to the gardaí, and his certificate was renewed the following year in the ordinary way. But this treatment had a lingering effect on him. His pride was injured by the high-handed way he'd been treated by the gardaí, who by then had involved him in another incident that was to have lasting repercussions.

When the Abbeylara GAA club reached the Longford county football final in 1998, John was as proud as anyone else in the community. To celebrate the occasion, a local publican, William Crawford, borrowed a large wooden effigy of a goat from a friend, and this good-luck symbol was brought from Mayo to Abbeylara. It stood tall and impressive on top of a car transporter, displayed on our little village green opposite Crawford's pub. Bedecked in the Abbeylara team colours, the goat was an eye-catching sight and added to the excitement of the team's achievement in reaching the final.

Unfortunately, late on the night of 22 September, the entire mascot was destroyed by fire. Being made from wood and straw, it quickly burned to ash when it was set alight. This had a huge impact on the small community of Abbeylara. The larger-than-life effigy had captured the imagination of all those who saw it, and people were incensed over this act of vandalism. It was also quite valuable, costing upwards of £2,000. Perhaps it was a sense of collective guilt that the mascot had been burned while in our village that made it such a talked-about incident and added to people's anger.

John was in Crawford's pub with some friends on the night in question. He walked home alone, but William Crawford was informed by two people that John was responsible for the arson attack. John heard about this accusation the following morning and immediately reported to the garda station in Granard to declare his innocence. Later that afternoon, Rose answered the door to a uniformed guard. He asked to speak to John, who wasn't home at the time. The guard told her that John must report to Granard garda station as soon as possible.

Like most of the village, Rose had heard about the burning of the mascot, but her initial belief was that this visit was to do with the return of John's shotgun. When he returned home that evening, she passed on the message, and he set off immediately for Granard. She expected him home shortly afterwards, but there was still no sign of him three hours later.

John, also believing he was about to have his shotgun returned, discovered on his arrival at the station that he was still under suspicion as the arsonist. He was interrogated by Garda Bruen for three hours and put into a cell. His belt and shoelaces were removed. Garda McHugh, a second guard, occasionally acted as a relief detective garda and was present during the interviewing. No notes were taken by either officer. Throughout the interrogation, John continued to protest his innocence and also mentioned the fact that his shotgun had been taken from him by subterfuge. He was detained from 7:36 p.m. until 10:35 p.m., then officially released without charge.

He was furious when he rang me in Galway and told me about his experience. I was deeply shocked by what I heard, especially his allegation that he'd been physically assaulted while in garda custody. Throughout my life, I'd taken the gardaí for granted. I'd given them my automatic trust, believed they'd be there if ever I needed them. Now, listening to John, hearing the anger as well as the fear in his voice, I was having serious second thoughts. He was worried that the arson charge would be made to stick and, knowing that the incident would quickly become local knowledge, feared the effect the publicity would have on Rose.

The following day, he attended Dr Cullen's surgery complaining of a neck injury. The doctor sent him to hospital for X-rays. No broken or dislocated bones showed up on the X-ray results, but Dr Cullen believed he'd sustained soft-tissue injury.

John wasn't responsible for burning the mascot and was never officially charged with this act of vandalism. Those who carried it out were two so-called friends who made no attempt to stand up for him and seemed quite content to allow him to take the blame. Shortly afterwards, while he was still seething about this incident, he found out the true reason his gun had been confiscated. From then on, he made no secret of his animosity towards the local gardaí. As he was the only person arrested over the destruction of the goat mascot, he was teased or told off regularly about it in the local pubs. Despite his denials, a number of people continued to blame him and believe he was responsible.

As Christmas drew near, these two incidents were still bothering John. We planned to spend the holiday together in Galway. I was looking forward to showing off my culinary skills and entertaining my mother for a change, instead of the other way around. My apartment was bright with fairy lights, my presents were wrapped, the turkey prepared. As soon as John arrived, though, I knew something was wrong.

Those of us who live with a loved one suffering from a bipolar disorder are familiar with the symptoms that can develop during an episode. These symptoms vary with individuals, but in John's own words, when he was heading into an elated state, he became impatient, argumentative and demanding. Everything had to be done instantly. I could see the restlessness in his eyes, his voice running away with words, his changeable mood. John's illness was episodic, not ongoing. For much of the time, he was his usual caring self, but when he was afflicted by an attack, it was difficult to slow him down. He told me he hadn't been sleeping well and found it difficult to concentrate on anything for more than a few minutes. Rose looked strained and tired. She loved him to distraction and worried about his fragile health. She told me he hadn't recovered from the mascot accusation and had cried on a number of occasions when the verbal abuse from certain people in the community really got to him. From talking to John, I understood how easily his self-esteem could be stripped away. Even small incidents could cause him to become stressed out and broody. I had suspected there would be fall-out from the two incidents, and I was now witnessing the results at first hand.

There was a hollow ring to our good cheer, but somehow we managed to get through Christmas Day. By St Stephen's Day, John knew he was too ill to continue without medical attention. He was acutely aware that this type of elated behaviour caused great distress to those closest to him and was rational enough to seek help.

Rose and I went with him to University College Hospital Galway, where he was admitted for treatment. After a few days, his elated mood stabilised. I was always surprised at how quickly his usual friendly personality returned. He was discharged twelve days later and stayed on with me in Galway, where he attended a psychiatric day hospital. He received the support and help he required, and when finally discharged, he was fully back to his normal self. His hospital records showed he'd been suffering a mild attack of elation. He had shown no suicidal urges or psychotic features.

John followed up this hospitalisation with a visit to Dr Shanley, who prescribed Stelazine and lithium, which would control his bouts of elation. He continued to visit me and, as I had done when I first came to Galway, he fell in love with the relaxed atmosphere of the city. In March 1999, he decided to move to Galway and find employment in the construction industry. To help him cope, he contacted an Aware branch operating in the city and attended their meetings. The consultations with Dr Shanley continued, and his medication was monitored. He found his own place to live and was employed as a plasterer, working for a while with a neighbour from home whom he liked. When this work ended, he worked on a new shopping centre which was being built in the city. He was sleeping well, watching his drinking and taking only a few pints when he was out with friends. The importance of controlling his alcohol intake was vital, as alcohol could affect his medication. Life was on a steady path again. I saw him every day, met the new friends he'd made, including Pepper and a young man called Kevin Ireland. Many of these friends had no idea he suffered from depression. They saw an affable young man who enjoyed having a laugh and a bit of fun with his mates.

Over the years, John had regularly gone out with girls. As his awareness of the symptoms of his illness grew, he became wary of forming romantic relationships. This changed early in the year of the new millennium when he met and fell in love with a young woman. They had much in common and enjoyed each other's company. Soon they were meeting on an almost daily basis. Seeing him so happy, I prayed he would walk that fine line between the two terrors in his life, depression and elation. For a short, happy time, it was possible to forget the shadow hanging over him and to believe that this contented phase would turn into something more lasting. He, too, allowed himself to hope things would work out but, sadly, this relationship, which had seemed so promising in the beginning, ended after a couple of months when he began to display signs of an impending bipolar episode.

Around the same time, he had decided to change jobs. The main reason was due to a disagreement with another employee on the site. While he was serving out his notice, the working situation between John and his co-worker deteriorated even further. John complained to his boss, but this action led to his dismissal. He was annoyed at being let go under what he considered to be unfair circumstances and mounted an unofficial picket outside the site. Worried about the legality of his one-man picket, he gave Kevin Ireland a piece of paper on which he'd written the name of a solicitor, Michael Finucane, with a Dublin address and telephone number.

The dispute was eventually sorted out with his employer, and Kevin gave the paper with the telephone number back to John. Only a few months later, the name of this solicitor would have deep significance for many people, but at the time, none of us had any indication that John's illness would take such a drastic turn. The problems in work affected his mood and spilled over into his relationship with his girlfriend. I could see that he was under stress and she, unaware that John suffered from a complicated illness, was unable to cope with this restless, possessive, demanding young man. She made a decision to end their relationship and not to see him again. Despite John's effort at reconciliation, she did not change her mind.

Chapter Four

Toneymore
Abbeylara
Co. Longford

Dear _____,
I do not want to get you into trouble with your boss, by phoning you at work, I just want to let you know, that I am missing you and let you know how I feel about you.

You know that I believe that a person should not be with someone unless they love them, as I do you. I hope you feel the same, furthermore whatever decision you make I will respect it and will not be pestering you. I think too much of you to upset you any further. I give you my deepest apology for the upset and annoyance I have put you through.

I haven't told you this before but due to the fact that from time to time I get elated (high) has caused me not to get deeply involved with someone until I met you. You are the first I told about this problem I have. I have been perfect for quite some time and I'm fine again thank God. I am sure you can understand somewhat . . . The way I have been acting in the last few weeks has put a lot of strain both on you and those closest to me. Marie in particular has been very upset and my friendship with 'Pepper' has been put under strain. To them I owe a lot. But it is you, ____, I have hurt most and it is this that upsets me most.

I do not wish to use this problem as an excuse for my behaviour but it is this that has made me so impatient and argumentative and so overbearing over the last while. I admire you for your honesty and you should always be in the future as trust is always best, in the long run.

I am sure we would be still together were it not for me being elated and my mood swings. Being elated has never got me into trouble really but if it means that I have lost you, it has been very costly and ruined my happiness.

When I am 'high' everything, must in my mind, be instant. Although it is usually a pleasurable experience being elated causes a lot of frustration for loved ones. As for my feelings at the moment. I have never been as happy with anyone before and I hope all is not lost.

It seemed to me to be the real thing, 'I never thought love could feel so good'. I told you on numerous occasions that I would be honest with you and I mean every word I say.

I feel something this good only comes along once in a lifetime and I hope all is not lost. My friends could not understand why I was so happy when I met you, they didn't realise how much you meant to me and you still do. With the elation goes big ideas, racing thoughts that has left me impatient. I hope you understand. My mood is fine now due to the emptiness and sadness due to missing you.

Maybe I don't deserve a second bite at the cherry but I believe everyone deserves a second chance. The way I have been acting irrationally over the past few weeks hasn't happened for five years up until now. So while it has caused a lot of hassle to both you and Marie it is not a persistent problem and I hope you can take this into consideration.

Maybe we could meet to have a chat. I think we owe that to each other. I will be in Galway probably next Wednesday or Thursday. Maybe we could meet then 'hopefully'.

I hope this letter gives you some idea of how I still feel about you. I hope it also gives you some explanation of the reason for my out of character behaviour which led to this situation.

No matter what has happened you still mean everything to me and I hope we can sort things out. By the way I hope you had a good weekend.

Your happiness is most important to me and I mean that. I could write all night but what I have written, means something to you, hopefully. It's now 1:50 a.m. I should go to bed.

Missing you more than words can say. Love John XXX

John was deeply upset over the way his relationship had ended. Shortly afterwards, unable to cope with his disappointment, he arranged to meet myself and Pepper to talk things over in the Goalpost Bar, our local pub. He had been drinking before we arrived. I was always anxious about him mixing alcohol with his medication, but on this night his mood seemed stable and sober. We decided to go to another pub in the city which was a favourite place for linking up with friends. Cullinane's was crowded and noisy, the atmosphere hyper. I knew as soon as we entered that this was exactly the wrong kind of environment for John. He was spilling out his feelings to us while at the same time being distracted by the noise, the flash of the television, the crush of bodies. When he went to the bar to order drinks, he pushed against another customer to make space. The customer elbowed him back, and the two of them started shuffling against each other. It was stupid, headstrong behaviour on both their parts and had the potential to flare into a serious row, especially when they began to exchange heated words. To add to John's annoyance, the barman, sensing trouble, asked us to leave the pub.

I decided the wisest course of action was to have something to eat. This would calm John down, and then we'd call it a night. We made our way to Supermac's in Eyre Square. By then, John was elated and agitated, his mood swinging one way and another. The city was full of boisterous young people spilling from bars, crowding the streets. With John in this elated state, it was a dangerous place to hang around. His giddiness, bravado and loud conversation could easily be mistaken by strangers as aggression, and a fight could start. I wanted him safely back in my apartment, but he was determined to stay out.

As his mood continued to fluctuate and more attention was drawn to us, I grew increasingly uneasy. Finally, I decided to take matters into my own hands. It was essential for John's safety that he see a doctor and get treatment to calm him down as soon as possible. Two gardaí, a man and woman, were on duty in Eyre Square. Pepper came with me to ask for assistance. I've no doubt the gardaí have certain straightforward procedures in place for dealing with a drink or drugs situation. Dealing with mental illness, however, is a different matter and much more complex than I'd realised.

At first, they were reluctant to become involved. I kept explaining the seriousness of the problem and pleaded with them to do something immediately. The female garda explained that John could go voluntarily to the psychiatric unit in a general hospital or, if he refused, I would have to commit him involuntarily under the Mental Treatment Act 1945 to Ballinasloe Psychiatric Hospital. It was my understanding that when someone was signed into a psychiatric hospital by another person, the patient could not be released unless signed out again. I would never have dreamed of signing John into a psychiatric hospital. I must have looked as worried as I felt because the garda agreed to come with us to Supermac's and talk to John.

At first we couldn't find him. I was afraid he'd taken off, but he soon emerged from the toilets. Eventually I agreed that he should be arrested under the Mental Treatment Act 1945, and he was brought to the garda station in Mill Street to be examined by a doctor. John was angry with me for involving the guards, but I ignored his complaints. All that concerned me was his personal safety.

A woman doctor was called to the station to examine him. She agreed that he was 'slightly elated', a common complaint with people suffering from manic depression. She wasn't worried that he was suicidal. John admitted to her that he was stressed, and she advised him to see his own doctor in the morning. By then he'd calmed down and thanked her for her assistance. His manner was courteous, without any of the earlier signs of distress. He was released into my custody. We returned to my apartment, but he remained annoyed with me for a few days afterwards. When his mood had fully stabilised, he thanked me and agreed that it had been the best course of action under the circumstances.

After the end of his relationship, John picked himself up and tried to get on with life. He decided to leave Galway for a while and return to Abbeylara, where a new house was being built for Rose. Once he arrived home, he sought work as a plasterer and secured a job in Longford town. We spoke to each other regularly on the phone and planned his move back to Galway, which would take place after Rose settled into her new house. It was almost ready – all that was left to organise was the power connection.

For three generations, the old cottage, which was built in 1906, had been in the Carthy family. Rose had moved into it when she married my father, and John's happiest years, before his depression set in, had been spent within its walls. But it was in need of constant repair, and an agreement had been made with the Local Authority for a new house to be built beside it on condition that the old house be demolished as soon as the new house was complete.

Outwardly, John appeared to accept this decision. His main concern centred on when the new house would be ready and how he could help Rose move our possessions into it. Moving house is a stressful time even under normal conditions, but for John, who was going through a difficult personal period in his own life, the strain was proving too much. One weekend, he visited me in Galway to discuss the future. He had found accommodation in Pepper's house, and with so much construction going on in Galway, he would have no problem finding work. Everything was in place for his return, yet I continued to worry. His moods fluctuated too much. Sometimes he appeared happy at the thought of the new house, but other times he resented the fact that the old house had to be demolished.

I'd no idea how deeply conflicted and confused he was on this issue. Despite the deterioration of our old house, he sometimes talked about maintaining it and living there on his own. He'd first suggested this idea a couple of years previously when plans for the new house were being finalised. He'd even persuaded Rose to write to the County Council and see if this could be achieved. They were adamant the house had to be demolished, and I thought he'd forgotten this notion. He saw his future in Galway and wanted my mother to have a comfortable, modern home.

John was also afraid that his illness was spiralling towards another episode. He needed to see his psychiatrist and have his condition reassessed. Two weeks before Easter, he asked me to book an appointment for him with Dr Shanley. Holy Thursday afternoon was the soonest I could get an appointment for him. Rose would accompany him to St Patrick's Psychiatric Hospital in Dublin.

When I rang him during my lunch break on the Wednesday afternoon of 19 April 2000, there was nothing about our conversation that worried me unduly. I made the call from the public pay phone, and our conversation was interrupted a few times when the line went dead before I could get the right amount of coins into the machine. His mood over the previous weekend had been changeable. I knew he'd been drinking, and this mixture of medication with too much alcohol made him edgy and argumentative. His humour seemed to improve over the next few days, and when we spoke on that Spy Wednesday, he seemed in good form, full of plans for Pepper's first visit to Abbeylara. I was relieved he would have his consultation with Dr Shanley over before the weekend arrived.

But on that fateful Wednesday evening, something snapped or went dreadfully wrong with John. Perhaps it was the tenth anniversary of my father's death that tipped the balance, or the sight of the new house, then almost complete. He may have looked too hard around him at the old house where he'd spent such happy times before his illness struck. His future would have seemed as bright as a newly minted coin in those days, but it was tarnished now, dogged with moods that pulled him in too many directions, and perhaps he may have seen his home, like his dreams, reduced to rubble. We can only speculate; no one can really appreciate how or why the various problems in John's life came together on that particular occasion. The result was to trigger a serious manifestation of bipolar disorder which caused him to act in a most unfamiliar, dangerous and distraught manner.

Chapter Five

When first informed of the incident by Mrs Carthy, Garda Gorman contacted Superintendent Byrne, the area commander at Granard, who was then in Dublin attending a meeting in Garda Headquarters. It was arranged that Superintendent Shelly, the area commander in Mullingar, would take charge, pending Superintendent Byrne's arrival later that night. The former agreed to do so and set about assembling a detachment of ten armed detectives recruited from various stations in the general area and also a group of unarmed uniformed gardaí. Superintendent Shelly's plan was to mount an armed cordon around the Carthy house to contain the gunman, and to use uniformed officers to set up roadblocks to prevent traffic from entering the area and also to patrol outlying fields to forestall members of the public from approaching the scene. Occupiers of houses in the immediate vicinity were also moved elsewhere for their safety.

The foregoing plans comprised an appropriate immediate response to the situation and were put in place. However, a practical difficulty was that neither Superintendent Shelly nor Superintendent Byrne, who rotated as scene commanders, had prior experience of dealing with any form of armed siege or with dangerous conduct which was motivated by mental illness. The local armed officers had no such experience either. This problem was averted to by Chief Superintendent Tansey *and Assistant Commissioner Hickey, the area superiors of the scene commanders. They decided that it was advisable to obtain the benefit of assistance from the Emergency Response Unit, a specialist body which is specifically trained in dealing with armed siege situations. However, the ERU also had no training in contending with a dangerous armed person motivated by mental illness. Detective Inspector (now Superintendent) Hogan of the ERU dispatched to Abbeylara a unit of six officers who were fully armed and equipped to deal with a siege situation. All had been already on duty elsewhere that day. The group comprised a tactical unit of four men under Detective Sergeant Russell; Detective Sergeant (now Superintendent) Michael Jackson as negotiator and Detective Garda (now Detective Sergeant) Sullivan, whose function was to assist the latter as messenger and note-taker. Sergeant Jackson had no prior experience as a siege negotiator, but in the previous month had attended a two-week negotiation course organised by the London Metropolitan Police relating to siege situations involving armed criminals with hostages and crisis intervention. Garda Sullivan had no training in negotiation.*

– Barr Tribunal report, Chapter 8: Conclusion, Section F: The Response of the Garda Síochána at Abbeylara

Life can change in an instant. With a click of your fingers or the blink of an eyelid, without warning, the world we take for granted suddenly shatters, and nothing is ever the same again. My life changed for ever when my phone rang on a rainy Wednesday evening and I heard my cousin Ann on the other end of the line. After the journey in the squad car, I had expected to make immediate contact with John. This had been refused and I was consumed with anxiety as I waited in Devines' house for the guards to return and collect me.

Outside, a media scene was unfolding. I'd experienced a breakneck journey from Salthill in a squad car and witnessed a police cordon surrounding my house. In Ballywillian I'd been interviewed by a member of the Emergency Response Unit especially brought to the scene from Dublin. The enormity of the situation was like a slow-moving fog that came over me every time I tried to see my way through it. Only one thing mattered: making contact with my brother.

My friend Patricia Leavey had been in the house waiting for me when I arrived back with Pepper from Ballywillian. Thomas also came into Devines' for a while. As I introduced Pepper to everyone, I thought back to my conversation with John earlier that day. How could we possibly have imagined that Pepper's first introduction to his friends would have been made under such extraordinary circumstances?

Mrs Devine busied herself preparing tea and sandwiches. She made a tray of hot whiskeys to take the chill from our bones, and I accepted one. In the warm, comforting atmosphere of her home, it seemed unbelievable that such frightening events were taking place only a short distance up the road. The relief of being with people who knew and understood John was overwhelming. We talked about him, tried to figure out the reasons for his unexpected behaviour. Everyone agreed that the presence of so many guards around the house was making things even more difficult.

As the conversation continued, we kept reminding ourselves that he would never hurt anyone. I sensed the apprehension my friends tried to hide behind their smiles of reassurance, but I was confident, despite my fears, that John had no inclination to harm himself. Suicidal or self-harming urges had never been a factor in the bipolar episodes he experienced.

Patricia spoke again about her efforts to contact him. She was sure he'd been listening, but she'd been unable to persuade him to talk. This was unpredictable behaviour, and I only hoped I'd succeed in getting him to listen to me. After we'd talked ourselves around in circles and were still no nearer to understanding what was going on, Patricia told us about her six-week holiday in Australia. I could see that she was in another time zone, having only returned that day. Despite the bitterly cold weather, she was wearing light summer clothes and sandals. Even this shift in our conversation was unreal, a determined attempt to normalise an abnormal situation and keep reality at bay.

The minutes ticked on. We were now into the small hours of the morning. Pepper was also becoming increasingly worried. We tried to figure out what to do but felt helpless. A checkpoint blocked off the entrance to the Toneymore Road, and I knew we wouldn't be allowed to go beyond it without garda permission.

It was after two in the morning when we were finally contacted. I would later discover that the guard who drove us back to Devines' house had gone on a refreshment break and hadn't informed the scene commander of our whereabouts, hence their delay in finding us. That such a fundamental piece of information could have been omitted never entered my mind as I walked up the road with Patricia and Pepper. Within a few minutes, we reached Aunty Nancy's house, which had earlier been evacuated. We weren't allowed to proceed any further. An inner and outer cordon of police still surrounded John. Guards in flak jackets and helmets were bleak shapes looming out of the shadows. If anything, the scene looked even more threatening. A single spotlight shone directly towards the kitchen, where John was conducting the stand-off. The noise from the generator was clearly audible. From my vantage point, I was unable to see over the bushes into the garden or into my house, but I was familiar with every step of the way. I'd seen the new house take shape, but now the evacuated earth was a barrier providing cover for guards who crouched behind, their guns aimed and ready. Jeeps were parked along the side of this leafy road with its cluster of bungalows where neighbours usually dropped in and out to each other for a chat and a cup of tea. The garden pillar had become the negotiation point. Behind it, armed and alert, the negotiator was a hunched shape.

We'd played on those pillars, jumped from one to the other, leaned against them chatting to friends, whitewashed them, walked between them without ever really noticing them. To see this familiar scene turned into something so shadowed and ominous was terrifying. John was surrounded and watched from every angle. I pictured the familiar surroundings of our kitchen, harshly exposed in the glare of the spotlight, eyes staring in at him as he struggled to figure out what to do next. I imagined his fear and confusion. His actions had taken on their own momentum, and he was now trying to deal with the consequences. So far, no one had been harmed, but I was under no illusions about the seriousness of the situation. I forced the future from my mind and concentrated on what I would say to him.

We were told by Superintendent Byrne, who had taken over from Superintendent Shelly as night scene commander, that John had requested to speak only to Pepper. I wouldn't be permitted near the scene. It was too dangerous, the superintendent stated. I kept my voice as steady as possible and told him it was essential I make contact with John. He insisted it wasn't going to happen, not at this moment. When the time was right, it would be organised. His comments, so vague and non-committal, increased my anxiety. Many of the uniformed gardaí close to this so-called 'dangerous' zone were unarmed. Were they and Pepper not also in danger? Why were only men making these decisions? Nothing about the scene made any sense. I could be flinging words into the wind for all the attention being paid to my opinions.

I watched as Pepper was introduced to Detective Sergeant Jackson, the appointed negotiator with the ERU. The negotiator was attempting to communicate with John through a megaphone. As Pepper headed towards the house, I could stand the strain no longer. I tried to get past Superintendent Byrne. He pushed me out of the way and blocked me again when I tried to move past him on his other side. I was ordered to sit in a garda jeep with Patricia and wait until Pepper came back. The superintendent had an air of authority about him. His word was law.

Once inside the jeep, I forced myself to calm down. Inwardly, I was sick with fear and frustration. I was so close to my brother yet separated by cordons of police who knew nothing about him or seemed to understand that his illness was already outside his control. Always in the past John had turned to me when he was in distress. At this dangerous, critical time in the small hours of the morning, I knew how much he needed to hear my voice. I wanted to run from the jeep and stand beside Pepper, but I knew it would be impossible to break through the ranks of gardaí.

Pepper stood behind the garden post and spoke to John through the loudhailer, reminding him of the good times they'd shared. He tried to reassure him that no one wished him harm. His voice would have sounded different, disembodied, the words floating towards John on the powerful beam of light. No answering voice came from the house. Eventually, bitterly disappointed, Pepper had to abandon his efforts.

When we returned to Devines' house, I tried to figure out the reasons for John's lack of response. He had asked to speak to Pepper earlier, so why had he remained silent when he heard a friendly voice? Had he grown tired waiting for Pepper to arrive, unaware that the gardaí were unable to find us? Pepper told me he'd been advised by the negotiator about what he should say. Although he'd tried to put these suggestions into his own words, had he sounded contrived, unlike his natural self? Remembering the harsh sound of the loudhailer, did John even believe it was Pepper, or was he convinced it was some kind of subterfuge being played out by the gardaí? In his heightened state of mind, anything was possible. We could do nothing except endure what was left of the night and hope that tomorrow would bring an end to the stand-off. I slept in Devines' house, although sleep is not the right word for the fitful dozing and waking, the worried tossing and turning, the frantic thoughts that haunted me as I counted down the hours until morning.

Chapter Six

On the morning of Wednesday, 19 April 2000, I was at home with my son, John. We got up in the morning, had something to eat and we were talking away as usual. We were in the house all day. John then started saying that no one was going to put him out of his house. We had been notified by the council that they would knock our old house when we went into the new one. John was against this and he wanted to hold the old house. He wanted me to go and live in the new house and he would stay in the old one. He was on about this and then at about twenty to four he went down to the locker in the hall where his gun was locked away. He came back to the kitchen and he had his gun with him. He also had a full box of cartridges and his gun belt. He was saying that no one was going to put him out of his house, that he was going to stay and I could move to the new house. He then loaded the gun with two cartridges in our kitchen and went outside to the hall door and let two shots go. He came back and sat beside the range in the kitchen. He had the gun with him and the cartridges. I was afraid that he might harm himself with the gun. I said I was going 'up to céilí' with my sister, that meant that I would go up and visit my sister, Mrs Nancy Walsh, who lives two doors up the road. He said goodbye and I went out and he hadn't loaded the gun. He didn't throw me out of the house either, like the papers said. I was always there for him and he was fond of me.

I went up to my sister, Nancy Walsh, and walked in. It was John I was worried about when I went in. There I met my niece, Ann Walsh, Alice Farrell, my neighbour and my sister, Nancy. I told them my son, John, was below in the house with the gun and the cartridges and I was worried that he might do some harm to himself. I asked them to ring the guards in Granard as I wanted them to come out and take the gun from John. I spoke on the phone myself to a lady guard and told her what had happened . . .

– Extract from Rose Carthy's statement

At eight o'clock the following morning, Alice Farrell drove Patricia, Pepper and myself to my cousin Trisha's house. When we arrived, I could see the worry and exhaustion on Rose's face. She is a quiet, dignified woman who cherishes her privacy. Now, suddenly, she was in the eye of a storm, reported in the media as having been ordered at the point of a gun from her house by her son. Terrified that John was going to harm himself, she had sought the help of the police, but somehow this simple request for assistance led to a stand-off situation. In an effort not to cause her any further distress, Trisha was keeping the radio and television off, but what we all found most upsetting as the day progressed was the lack of firm information from the gardaí. Rose had been interviewed by a guard before my arrival, and had given him as much detail as she could about the situation. A young female guard, who was still a probationer, was appointed to act as a liaison officer between us and the gardaí. Although pleasant and sympathetic, she too was unable to provide us with any solid information. Without recourse to radio or television, I checked the Aertel service. It was there I discovered that John had asked for cigarettes. Knowing his nicotine addiction, I assumed these had been given to him.

Time dragged by as we waited for the summons to return to Abbeylara. My cousins came and went. Ann, who had been in the village, was shocked by the amount of media on the scene. She had spoken to Superintendent Farrelly and warned him that the coverage would have a detrimental effect on John. She asked for a media blackout, but her request was not granted.

As I tried to console Rose and waited impatiently to be brought to John, I tried to piece together the sequence of events that had led to this terrifying situation.

Those who were with Rose in Nancy's house on that Wednesday afternoon knew that John was not an aggressive person. They were more worried about his own safety than any harm he would do to them. Both Alice Farrell, our neighbour, and Ann had been talking to him during the previous few days. He'd told them he was bored in Abbeylara and was looking forward to settling Rose into the new house so that he could head back to Galway. He was his usual self, in good form as he chatted away about his future.

On the Tuesday before the stand-off, when Alice called to our house to talk to my mother, John had seemed slightly elated and made a comment about the guards not coming around to the house any more. He also said something similar to Ann. He was calm when he made this remark, and she formed an opinion that someone could have been teasing him about sending the guards to arrest him again. She was John's godmother and they had a close, friendly relationship. Knowing that he had an appointment with Dr Shanley in two days' time, she wasn't too worried about his comment, but now, faced with such a fraught situation, it was obvious that he needed professional help before things got out of hand.

It was decided the best course of action was to ring the guards and explain the situation. Rosaleen Mahon, another of my cousins, arrived and decided to ring Dr Cullen. He knew John's history and would be able to pass on essential medical information to the guards.

Two guards from Granard Station, Garda Gibbons and White, were sent to the scene. Garda Gibbons was armed. Before trying to make contact with John, they called to my aunt's house, where they were notified about his depression. They were also informed that John had a particular animosity towards the guards in Granard because of the goat-mascot accusation. The guards, having received the relevant information, then drove up the driveway of our house in their patrol car. The sight of the car obviously frightened or antagonised John. Either way, he reacted by firing two shots from the house. Again, these were not aimed in any direction, but the guards quickly reversed back down the driveway and out of sight.

Back on the Toneymore Road, they spoke briefly to Dr Cullen, who had arrived before them and parked nearby. Dr Cullen also reiterated that John had a problem with the guards and gave them details about his bipolar disorder. This conversation was brief and now, looking back with so much hindsight, I wonder how the complexities of such a serious illness could have been explained and understood in just a few minutes.

Another guard, Detective Garda Campbell, arrived in an un-marked car. He, too, was armed. Garda White stayed with Dr Cullen, while Garda Gibbons got into the unmarked squad car with Detective Garda Campbell. They parked close to the old house and went around the gable end. Garda Campbell knocked on the front door and asked John if he was all right. John's animosity towards the guards once again proved too much for him – he shot from the window. The guards were close enough for him to aim in their direction, but he made no effort to do so. Instead, he aimed at the empty squad car and damaged the wing. The guards then retreated under cover and abandoned the car in the driveway with the keys in the ignition. These keys were now within John's reach should he have decided to leave the house. But he stayed where he was, alone and in the grip of an increasingly serious bipolar attack.

Shortly afterwards, Superintendent Shelly arrived on the scene and formed an armed cordon of guards around the house. Efforts were made to talk to John using the loudhailer. This proved to be a poor method of communication, and he made no effort to respond. As reports went up the chain of command, the decision was made to call in the ERU. The confrontation had begun.

We kept our thoughts to ourselves as we moved through the hours of Holy Thursday; to voice them aloud was too terrifying. It's difficult to describe the sensation of being unable to help someone in distress. I was reminded of my father's final illness and how ineffective I'd felt as he lay dying and I could do nothing to ease his pain. Ten years ago, on a Holy Thursday, he had left us. My grandfather had also died on the same day. I refused to even contemplate the possibility that John would suffer the same fate. All I could do was pray the stand-off would end peacefully.

Many of my friends contacted me on my mobile to see if I was okay or if there was anything they could do to help. The only one thing I wanted was to speak to my brother, but the guards showed no signs of returning for me. I'd expected to be interviewed in depth, my opinion sought, my advice heeded. I now realise it was a naïve assumption, but at the time, I couldn't understand what was causing the delay.

After lunch, when there was still no summons, I refused to wait any longer. By now, I was frantic, determined to square up to the guards and insist on being allowed to speak directly to my brother. Accompanied by Pepper and Patricia, I left my mother and returned to the village. I had to find out for myself what was happening.

The afternoon was cold, wet and windy. Abbeylara was unrecognisable, filled with journalists, television and radio reporters. John was the focus of their attention. Hourly news bulletins about the unfolding events were being relayed across the nation. I sensed their excitement, the itch of a story, the desire for a scoop. Tomorrow there would be another story, and Abbeylara would return to its usual solitude.

Chapter Seven

Reporter: *Right now I am standing on the Toneymore Road, about 100 yards from the house. Any nearer and the gardaí say we are actually within range. As you know this man has fired some 20 shots over the past 24 hours. I have been down, the gardaí have allowed us down to the edge of the house but very warily, I assure you. There are about 32 houses on the road; it is a very long road. Gardaí have evacuated the nearest five families. There is an ambulance at the scene and a doctor has been around during the day. It is quite tense here, as I can tell you.*

Studio to reporter: *Tell us about the security response so far.*

Reporter: *Well, this man is armed, as I say, and he has a supply of shotgun ammunition. Hunting and fishing are very popular recreational pastimes in Abbeylara and it is quite usual for families to own a legally held firearm. Nevertheless, the gardaí, as they must, are treating this very seriously. Upwards of 60 gardaí have been moved into the area and about three dozen are on duty at any one time. There are trained negotiators at the scene, but what really strikes you when you see the house is the number of armed officers there are here, members of the Emergency Response Unit. There are also local detectives armed with Uzi sub-machine guns. When you look at the house and the area, helmeted figures in bulletproof vests hug the wall outside the house, the hedges above and around the site and the*

hills and valleys all around, and yet what they want is a
peaceful resolution to this tragic story . . .
  – RTÉ report

On the morning of Holy Thursday, cars were organised to transport cameramen, photographers, radio journalists and print journalists to the scene of the stand-off. The media were unable to see the house from where they gathered but were brought in relays to a spot where they could take photographs and make their reports. The camera crews went first, followed by photographers and then journalists. Each group was allowed to stay at the scene for approximately three minutes. They remained on the road for about twenty-five minutes before returning to the village.

Allowing them such close access to an armed operation must have made for powerful reality television, as images of the ERU in action were broadcast throughout the nation. But there's a bitter irony in the fact that twenty-five strangers were allowed within sight of my house whereas I, the individual closest to John in the world, was not allowed near its perimeter because of the so-called danger this would create. Later, when I heard about the consideration the media received from the guards, I compared it to the scant consideration given to my family and wondered what the end result would have been if we had not been left on the outer fringes of John's crisis.

That afternoon, when I returned to the village with Pepper and Patricia, we quickly made our way to the Devines' house. The Devine family couldn't believe the news that I hadn't been allowed contact with John. With their words of advice ringing in my ears, I set off again with Pepper. I avoided the film crews, having no intention of being caught on camera. If John saw me on television, it would destabilise him even further. I identified myself to the guard on checkpoint duty, and we were allowed up the Toneymore Road.

As had happened the previous night, we were only able to

approach as far as my aunt's house. The number of guards at the scene seemed even greater than the previous day. A garda jeep had become the command point from which decisions were made. It was now after four o'clock, and it was becoming obvious that the situation couldn't be contained much longer. The only response I got from the guards was the well-worn promise that communications were being organised. Each time I asked, the reply was the same.

Using my mobile phone, I again tried to phone John but was unable to get through. I later discovered that other people had had the same difficulties and am convinced John was switching his phone on and off as his mood fluctuated. He was so far gone on his own dark journey that he'd responded angrily when Thomas, one of the people he most liked and respected, had earlier tried to speak to him. He'd accused Thomas of not visiting him when he was in St Loman's Hospital, a fact we all knew to be untrue.

I heard for the first time that Dr Shanley, John's psychiatrist, had arrived in Abbeylara. It seemed like a lifetime ago since I'd contacted his clinic and made the appointment. By now, if all had gone according to plan, John would have had his consultation and his medication adjusted to help him stabilise. Now they would speak to each other over a loudhailer and through an armed police cordon.

Upon finishing work on Holy Thursday, Dr Shanley was due to leave for a short Easter break in the west of Ireland with his family. That morning, when contacted about John's situation, he'd decided to detour to Abbeylara. As soon as he reached Abbeylara, he went directly to Trisha's house to speak with my mother. I heard afterwards that Rose was too upset to add any further insights into her son's behaviour. He then left Coole Road and came directly to the scene.

Meanwhile, I was making further efforts to talk to John. I used a telephone provided by a guard. John's phone rang, but he didn't answer it. As I was using a different number, he wouldn't have understood that it was me who was trying to reach him. Thomas was also at the scene. Again, he'd been allowed to speak to John but, as on the previous occasion, he'd had no luck, nor had John's friend, Sean Farrell. Although I was glad efforts by his friends had been made to reach him, however unsuccessfully, I couldn't understand why I was still being kept away. I felt diminished, of no consequence to my brother's life.

I still wasn't aware of what had happened during the day. I would later discover that the cigarettes I'd assumed John had received had, in fact, become a bargaining tool in the negotiations. The guards claimed it was too dangerous to hand them over, yet in the small hours of the morning an opportunity arose to deliver them safely to him. It occurred when the tactical commander, Sergeant Russell, decided to remove the ignition keys from the garda car that had earlier been abandoned in the driveway. After this was successfully achieved, he checked the house. John had locked the front door, but there was no sign of activity from the kitchen window. Sergeant Russell kept out of sight as he approached the window. He discovered a small hole in the frame and peered through. John was sleeping on the couch, a rug pulled halfway up to his chest. He moved occasionally, his body jerking as if disturbed by nightmares. His gun was nowhere to be seen. It would have been easy to take that chance and leave the cigarettes on the window ledge where he would find them when he awoke. It might have made a significant difference to his mood, but the general view of the gardaí appeared to be that cigarettes could only be delivered with John's consent and cooperation.

I could hardly contain my relief when Dr Shanley arrived. Arrangements were being made for him to go down near the house and, finally, I was also given permission to speak to John. Another hour passed as we waited for this contact to be organised. I couldn't understand the delay. With as much calm as I could muster, I waited in a police car with Dr Shanley. I was with a professional who was prepared to listen to me and would hopefully help resolve the stand-off.

There is a picture in my mind of those moments that will never fade. I see the three of us – Pepper, Thomas and myself – sitting in the back seat. Dr Shanley is in the front. His voice is kind, reassuring. John is being informed through the loudhailer that I am here with his psychiatrist, waiting to speak to him. I hear shots but have no idea of their direction. I try to see what's going on, but the shoulders of the guards block my view.

A short while after this announcement, the guards suddenly begin to scatter, running frantically in different directions. Some of them duck for cover behind a police jeep. Another hides behind a wall. I still can't see what's causing the commotion. Blind panic sweeps through me. I hear voices calling, 'He's out! He's out!' I'm frozen to the seat of the car, unable to do anything except stare in horror towards the road outside my house.

I realise that John has finally emerged. I hear commands ringing out. He's being ordered to drop his gun. I hear the crack of bullets. But they don't come from John's shotgun. I rush from the car. I don't recall whether I scream or cry out. John is lying at the edge of the road opposite our house. He isn't moving. Blood is seeping from his body. I attempt to run past the guards. A garda pushes me back, tries to convince me that John is okay. I can tell by her expression that she is lying and plead with her to let me go to him. In my heart, I know my brother is dying. All I want to do is lie by his side and comfort him. He must not die among strangers in a pool of blood. I can feel him going from me, and there is nothing I can do except stand helplessly by and breathe out his last minutes with him. Since ten o'clock the previous night, all I'd asked from the gardaí was an opportunity to speak to my only brother. Now all I want is the opportunity to say my final goodbye. As John draws his last breath, I am not even permitted that right.

Chapter Eight

At approximately 5:55 p.m. John Carthy, without prior warning, exited his house through the front door. He was in possession of his shotgun, which he had in the broken-open position. He immediately turned to his left, walked down by the side of the house, rounded the corner, passed the gable end, paused momentarily at the next corner and proceeded down the driveway. As he passed through the gateway he closed the gun. Having moved on to the road he then opened the weapon, discarded one of two cartridges from it and closed it once more. He then turned up the roadway and proceeded to walk in the direction of Abbeylara with his shotgun closed, loaded with one cartridge and pointed in the direction of the command post, near which non-ERU members, armed and unarmed, were on the road. Moments later he lay fatally injured, having been shot four times by two members of the Emergency Response Unit.
  – Barr Tribunal report, 'The Final Minutes: John Carthy's Exit from the House and Subsequent Fatal Shooting', Section A: Introduction and Summary

At six o'clock, the Angelus bell rang out from St Bernard's Church and resounded across the fields and houses surrounding Abbeylara.

Today, hearing that call which summons us to pause and pray, my body shudders at the sound, and I think of John walking along the Toneymore Road for the last time.

The gardaí informed Pepper that my brother was dead. Stunned and unable to comprehend what had occurred, we tried to comfort each other. Pepper, Thomas and Dr Shanley surrounded me and supported me, but my heart was shattered, just as surely as John's body lay shattered on the roadside. Part of me went with him and has never returned.

An emergency ambulance raced to the scene. It had been parked three miles away in Granard instead of being positioned close by – not that it mattered how long it took to arrive. Like my brother's short life, the so-called Abbeylara siege was over. At 6:16 p.m., Fr Fitzpatrick arrived and administered the last rites. A GP from Granard, Dr Niall Donohoe, pronounced John dead at the scene. Shortly afterwards, gardaí preserved the scene and prevented unauthorised access until six o'clock on Easter Sunday evening.

Pepper and Thomas led me away from the heartbreaking chaos that surrounded my brother's death. I rang Devines' house, where Patricia Leavey was waiting for me. I wanted to break the news to her, but the person who answered my call thought I was asking for my cousin Trisha, who was standing outside the house. Trisha took the call, believing it was for her. I was in such a state of shock that it was a long time afterwards before I discovered that I'd been talking to my cousin, not Patricia, as I had believed. What I can recall most vividly is the sense of desolation as I left John's body behind me and headed back down the Toneymore Road.

In the village, cameras and reporters were everywhere. Trisha was insistent that Rose couldn't be told the news until a doctor was present. We were driven immediately to her house, where the dreadful news was broken to Rose. She had turned to the guards to protect her only son. Now she would mourn him for the rest of her life. As the media informed the nation that John had been shot dead, the local community of Abbeylara, who had planned to offer up an evening mass in the hope that the stand-off would end peacefully, gathered together to pray instead for the repose of his soul.

As word spread, my mobile phone kept ringing. Close friends contacted me to offer their sympathy and see if there was any way they could help. As we tried to grapple with the enormity of what had occurred, relations and neighbours formed a different cordon around us, an invisible one built from comfort and practical help. The value of real friends was very apparent at that difficult time. Their support was necessary to keep us going from one hour to the next.

It was announced on the evening news that the gardaí intended to investigate the circumstances surrounding John's fatal shooting. I was still too traumatised to absorb this announcement. There was much I needed to know, but until John's funeral was over, I didn't want anything to intrude on the preparations we were making to bury him with dignity and love.

Because the time of death was established, Dr Harbison, the State Pathologist, decided that John's body could be moved from the scene and brought to Mullingar General Hospital. At 10:20 p.m. that night, my brother was removed from the roadside and arrived at the hospital at 11:30 p.m. His body was taken to the X-ray department, then on to the post-mortem room. Dr Harbison commenced his examination at 9:38 a.m. on Good Friday morning. The post-mortem revealed that John had been shot four times. Thomas went to the hospital to perform the grim task of officially identifying John's body. I still recall him returning to us and admitting, 'He looked pretty bad.' I didn't want to hear any more.

Our immediate family and neighbours helped in every possible way to assist us in organising John's funeral. We found ourselves on a conveyor belt that seemed to move at a dreamlike pace through each stage of the proceedings. Somehow, without quite knowing how it happened, decisions were made, arrangements put in place, rituals organised. The abiding grief that must be endured usually hits hardest when the funeral is over and people have gone their separate ways. Grief then has its way in the quiet aftermath. But when a death is unexpected and has become a topic of discussion among the public and over the airwaves, there is little time to deal in private with one's loss. So it was with my brother's death.

His body had been taken from Mullingar Hospital to the mortuary in Our Lady's Manor Nursing Home in Edgeworthstown. So many people had gathered in the mortuary that I found it difficult to make my way to his coffin. I felt faint and had to sit down to recover. My friends from Galway and the village gathered around me, sympathising. John was laid out in a new shirt and trousers. He seemed peaceful, yet his body was cold and lifeless. Rosary beads had been threaded through his fingers. People began to pray. The sound rose and fell as decades of the rosary were recited. Everyone was in shock, many openly weeping. I couldn't believe this was actually happening. Soon I'd awaken and everything would be normal again. But reality was the sight of my mother's dazed, stricken face and the crush of people who had gathered to pay their last respects to John.

The grim, waiting silence bore down on me as people filed from the room of repose and left us alone with his body. Rose and I said our goodbyes before his coffin was closed. I touched his face and hands. His chest was bandaged up. Pepper and I carefully placed a pack of ten cigarettes in his pocket. It was too late now, but somehow it seemed important to give him this simple thing that had been denied him. Then we could linger no more. It was time to leave. As I escorted Rose to the waiting crowd of sympathisers, I felt her trembling and wondered how she was going to cope with all that awaited us in the future.

I travelled alone in the hearse with John for the 40-minute journey. With every familiar mile that passed, I thought of how he, too, had travelled this same journey ten years previously on the feast day of Good Friday with the body of our father in the coffin behind him.

His remains were brought to St Bernard's Church, the scene of so many joyful occasions: baptism, communions, confirmation, the weddings of friends, the chats after mass on Sunday mornings, the Easter liturgies and Christmas celebrations. Now, only a short distance up the road from where he was shot, John entered the church for the last time.

The weather remained cold and damp. Dark clouds bunched low over the village. Even people who never knew John or our family offered us their condolences on that dark Good Friday evening. Those who couldn't fit inside the church had to stay outdoors until the service was over. A primary-school photograph of John and I sat on top of his coffin. A thoughtful neighbour, Maura Newman, had placed it there. That picture still sits over the sitting-room fireplace in our new home, a reminder of happier times.

I cried throughout the entire service. All the emotions I'd experienced over the previous two days – the anger, frustration, terror and disbelief – had been replaced by an overwhelming grief that swelled inside me. It reached a point where I believed my chest could no longer contain the pain. I needed space to breathe. I had to leave the church during the service and go outside to gain the strength to continue.

The flow of sympathisers who queued to pay us their condolences seemed endless, but somehow it did end, and we left John in peace. The Catholic Church in Ireland doesn't permit burials on Easter Saturday, so his body remained in repose for two nights. As technical experts scoured the area, the sense of frustration and sadness felt by the quiet community of Abbeylara was intensified when we were informed on Good Friday evening that the long-standing Irish tradition of the funeral cortège pausing outside the house of the deceased would not be permitted – John was to be denied his final farewell.

On Easter Sunday morning, as the resurrection of Christ's body was being celebrated, we buried John. The reality of what had occurred was finally beginning to sink in, the pain becoming even more excruciating. Rose was in a complete trance as we went through the rituals of burial. I helped to carry John's coffin on my shoulders. The weight of it forced me to control myself as I walked down the main aisle. I was aware of the crowds, of friends reaching out, of tears and music and the beat of our footsteps as we walked in unison to the end of the church.

Just like the service on Good Friday night, the church was packed with mourners. The friends we had made in Galway were there in force, too many to greet or even notice among the congregation, but I'll never forget the comfort we gained from their numbers and from those strangers who took time off from their Easter break to share the day with us.

Because of the technical investigations being carried out at the scene of the shooting, our house remained cordoned off. We weren't allowed within its vicinity. Even the simple act of allowing Rose to collect clothes for her son's funeral was forbidden. Nothing was to be disturbed until a thorough investigation had been carried out.

A guard of honour was held outside the church as John's remains were taken on his short journey to our local cemetery, about 300 metres away. A chill wind blew around us as we walked up the narrow, leafy lane and laid him to rest beside my father. An Easter lily was thrown in on top of the coffin, followed by some red roses.

Photographers, who had swamped the village since the stand-off, were told by Thomas that their presence was too upsetting for our family and they were not welcome at the removal or burial, but I recall seeing journalists and a camera crew outside the church. At a certain level, I understood why they were present. From the moment the guards surrounded our house, the media had turned my brother's crisis into a huge story of national interest. Now they were there to witness and record its conclusion. A picture of us carrying out the coffin was printed in one of the newspapers. I saw it afterwards and remember thinking we were just another story, another day's work.

I often sit and wonder if my father came with open arms to meet John and give him the serenity he so desperately needed in this life. Maybe Patsy and my grandfather were also there to welcome him. I'd like to think that this is how it happens when a loved one dies. I'll never know the answer until I, too, pass on from this life.

Chapter Nine

It is pertinent to state also that Superintendent Shelly appears to have done very little, if anything, in his adopted role of intelligence co-ordinator. As far as the evidence goes, the only person who had meaningful contact with John Carthy during the entire siege was his friend, Kevin Ireland, who he phoned by mobile at about noon on 20 April, i.e. six hours before his death. The subject told his friend that he had no intention of shooting any garda officer or himself. He indicated that his purpose in firing his gun was to keep the ERU officers away from his house.

Superintendent Shelly and the negotiator learned about Mr Carthy's telephone conversation with Mr Ireland by way of an inaccurate and garbled fourth-hand version of it. Nothing was done about obtaining directly from Kevin Ireland a detailed account of his conversation as it ultimately emerged in evidence at the Tribunal.

– Barr Tribunal report, Conclusions

The only person John managed to contact during that long, drawn-out stand-off was Kevin Ireland, one of the friends he'd made when they were working together on a construction site in Galway. Kevin, who is a crane driver, was sitting with a friend in a lorry when John phoned him. Like the rest of the country, Kevin had been tuning in to the radio broadcasts and was astonished to hear John on the other end of the line. According to Kevin, John sounded calm. He said he was alone in the house and surrounded by 'sixty cowardly guards'. It was obvious he was listening to the radio and knew that the stand-off was national news. Kevin pleaded with him not to do anything stupid like shooting himself or anyone else. John replied that he hadn't a notion of firing at anyone. He had broken nearly every window in the house and was firing his gun as a warning to the guards to keep away. He asked Kevin not to tell the gardaí he had been in touch. When Kevin asked him to give himself up, John told him to contact a solicitor called Mick Finucane. Then he abruptly ended the phone call. Kevin tried to phone him back, but his call remained unanswered.

Kevin was torn between John's request that he shouldn't inform the police and his own belief that they should know what had occurred. Anxious about the responsibility placed on him and nervous in case he unwittingly made the situation worse if John heard he had been in contact with the guards, he rang his mother, Mary, for advice. She advised him to inform the police. Mary worked in Shannonside Radio and rang the station to alert them to John's phone call. Shannonside Radio immediately contacted Noeleen Leddy, a journalist who was working for the station at that time. Noeleen was covering the events at Abbeylara and was in the village awaiting developments with the rest of the media. As soon as she received this information, she was admitted through the garda checkpoint and brought to the scene. She informed the press officer, Superintendent Farrelly and Superintendent Shelly about John's phone call and his request for a solicitor. She also gave them Kevin's mobile number so that they could phone him back and check the details.

Kevin tried on a number of occasions to ring John back, but without any success. Eventually, two hours later, when he was unable to contact him and had heard nothing from the guards, he called into the garda station in Mill Street, Galway. From there, his information was passed on to Sergeant Monahan at Granard garda station, who then passed it on to Superintendent Shelly. Sergeant Monahan tried to identify the solicitor John requested by checking the 01 telephone directory but was unable to find him. The guards at the scene made no effort to contact Kevin and discover in detail what John had said.

Nor was any effort made by the guards to check with John's family to see if we could help with information. We would have been unable to throw any light on Michael Finucane's identity, but could have given them vital information about our own family solicitor, Frank Gearty. I already had given the gardaí his name when I was being interviewed in Ballywillian and had assumed they'd made contact with him during Holy Thursday. No contact was ever made with Frank, nor did the gardaí discover the identity of Michael Finucane until shortly before John left the house. By then it was too late.

Michael Finucane is the son of Patrick Finucane, the high-profile Belfast solicitor shot dead in 1989 at his home in front of his family. At the time of John's stand-off, Michael was a trainee solicitor working in Dublin. A phone call to the Law Society would have easily identified him. As John sank deeper into his depression and agitation, another opportunity to control the situation was lost. I often wonder if John would have been given more credence if he had been an ordinary criminal or a hardened terrorist. Were his demands defined by his illness? Were his requests not taken seriously because of his history of depression and his demented behaviour at the scene?

During his conversation with Kevin, he claimed his family 'wouldn't even get him a solicitor'. This comment was, and still is, deeply upsetting. It showed his delusional state of mind as he struggled to extricate himself from an impossible situation.

Kieran Lennon, another friend and workmate of John's, also attempted to ring him on a number of occasions. His first call to John went unanswered, but at 3:30 p.m. he was finally successful. Kieran heard music playing in the background. John sounded calm as he informed him that he was busy and would have to hang up. As the stand-off drew to its fatal conclusion, he became increasingly distraught. He was heard shouting, 'Why, why, why?' and banging the butt of his rifle off the furniture. By that stage, his identity was known, his name broadcast. Local people had been interviewed, asked personal questions about his private life, his family, their views on the stand-off. Over the following days, I listened to these interviews, sickened by the knowledge that John may have heard his name and these personal details being disclosed over the radio. Why had the gardaí not demanded a media blackout until the stand-off was resolved? Perhaps that was the reason John left the house. Perhaps his need for cigarettes drove him into the open. Maybe he was coming to meet me or to surrender. No one will ever know why he walked up the Toneymore Road to meet his death.

He was wearing jeans, a padded navy-blue jacket and a football shirt. On the driveway where the surface was stony, he broke his shotgun in case it misfired. Once he was on a smooth surface, he closed it again. The butt was tucked under his right arm, his right hand in the trigger area and the barrel was supported by his left hand. The gun was never held at shoulder height, nor did he point it at any member of the ERU at any stage, even though he walked right past the men who were calling on him to drop his gun. I wonder if he even heard them.

After crossing the road, he released one cartridge from the double barrel and continued walking towards the jeep that had served as a command post throughout the stand-off. One cartridge remained in his gun. He was shot from behind. The first bullet entered the inside of his left thigh and exited also on the inside of the left thigh. The second bullet also entered and exited his left thigh, slightly above the first wound. When the third bullet was fired, it entered the base of his spine and exited at the scrotum. The fourth bullet hit his lower back, travelled upwards, forwards and to the left, and exited the left side of the chest, just above the left nipple. He also had two lacerations on the back of the right calf, which appeared to be re-entry and exit wounds from the bullet that exited his left thigh. The gardaí claimed that he continued moving as they shot him. They said he maintained his 'purposeful and menacing walk' even with three bullets inside him. It took a fourth bullet to bring him down.

Chapter Ten

This last week has been a tragic one for my family, the Abbeylara community and all John's friends. Those who knew John best know that he was intelligent, popular, hardworking, witty, gentle and never let anyone down.

Like so many people worldwide, John had experienced depression, but had come to terms with it and had learned how to deal with it.

I do not wish to blame anyone for what happened to John, but I wish to call for a searching independent inquiry and would like the results to be made public so that a tragedy like this will never happen again.

Finally, I would like my family, the Abbeylara community and John's friends to be allowed to grieve our loss. On behalf of my family, I would like to thank everyone who gave us support over the last week. I do not wish to answer any questions at the moment. Thank you for coming.

– My first public statement to the media

At first, it was impossible to know where to turn. With the help of friends and relatives, I tried to piece together the sequence of events leading to John's death. From newspaper clippings and discussions, a picture began to emerge. The more information I received, the more questions crowded my mind. Why had the guards not sought specialist medical advice more quickly? Why did they not give John the cigarettes he requested instead of using them as a bargaining tool to force him to negotiate? Why had the media been alerted so quickly? Why had his request to Kevin Ireland for a solicitor not yielded any results? Why was his name broadcast on *Five Seven Live*? Why was my family so badly informed throughout the entire stand-off? I also wondered – indeed, was haunted – by the knowledge that John had not phoned me at any stage during his ordeal. I would later find out that this was not the case, but at the time I was unable to prevent myself from feeling angry with him for ignoring me.

On the night he died, the news of an internal garda inquiry was announced on the evening news. Two investigations were underway. One involved the local gardaí, which is the usual procedure once a shooting of any sort takes place. But because of the nature of the Abbeylara stand-off, a special garda inquiry was announced. The findings, we were told, would not be made public. This increased my grief. There would be no answers for us, no accountability.

We were not the only people concerned with this announcement. The Fine Gael justice spokesman Jim Higgins said the results of the garda investigation must be made public and announced that he intended bringing the issue up in the Dáil when it resumed the following month. The Socialist Party deputy Joe Higgins was also demanding answers and called for the establishment of an independent inquiry alongside the garda inquiry. It was incomprehensible, he stated, that the expertise available to the gardaí had not made it possible to incapacitate John instead of shooting him dead.

Some of the media were still in Abbeylara. To avoid any unwanted publicity, Rose continued to stay on in Trisha's house, and the proprietor of the Park House Hotel in Edgeworthstown kindly offered rooms to me, Patricia and Pepper. When we arrived on Good Friday, he greeted us with open arms, even though his hotel was closed for business on that day. Both he and his staff were very supportive. Most of them knew John and willingly assisted me in any way they could as I tried to get my thoughts together. But even there, memories of John were in the bricks and mortar. A couple of years previously he'd carried out renovation work on the building. We'd often frequented the function room together at weekends when it featured the top bands and singers.

Information that should not have been in the public domain was already being printed about John. One of the Sunday newspapers told readers that John's gun had been confiscated and returned to him only after the guards received a letter from a medical expert claiming John was stable enough to handle it. No other information about the subterfuge surrounding the confiscation of his gun or the fact that he'd never had any previous incidents with it was included. If the media had bothered to interview members of the gun club, they would have discovered that John's safety record in the use of his shotgun was exemplary. The facts presented as they were painted a grim picture of a wild, out-of-control young man who was a danger to his community.

I sat in my hotel room feeling dazed and helpless, unable to stop weeping. The hotel proprietor, Frank Kilbride, was a rock of strength and practical advice. He suggested that the best way forward was to contact my family solicitor, Frank Gearty, and set up a meeting with him. When I arrived at his office in Longford town, he was equally sympathetic. This helped me to pull myself together and think about how I should go about defending John's reputation. After much discussion, I decided to go public and issue a press statement. The media were waiting for a response from the Carthy family, and it was becoming clear that it had to be organised sooner rather than later.

The thought of facing the media terrified me. John was the outgoing one, whereas I was quiet and more reserved. My lifestyle was simple – fun with my friends, dancing, concerts, a job I enjoyed. I had never sought the limelight, but now, less than a week since John was shot, I would have to sit in front of the assembled media and read a statement demanding a public inquiry from the State.

We organised the press conference in the Longford Arms Hotel in Longford town. Rose was still too traumatised to attend. Frank Gearty, Thomas and Pepper accompanied me. The conference room was filled with journalists, radio reporters and television crews. I was trembling as I faced the cameras. It was difficult to ignore the flashing lights and the photographers moving about as they shot from different angles. I sensed the curiosity of the journalists gathered, but apart from my prepared statement, I was not going to answer any questions. At that early stage, the ordeal would have been too much for me.

I tried to keep my voice steady as I read the short statement and somehow I managed to deliver it. As soon as I finished, we left the room. The press respected my grief and didn't intrude with any personal questions, but I knew in my heart that this was only the first of a number of times I would speak in public to defend John's reputation. So many people are afflicted with depression. It was too late for John, but I never wanted any other family to go through the agony we were suffering.

The people of Abbeylara were also deeply disturbed at the way the stand-off had been handled and the subsequent publicity. Everyone I met asked the same question: would the State cover up its mistakes? Soon after John's funeral, Peter O'Reilly and Vincent Quinn, two prominent and well-respected men in the community, decided that somebody had to stand up and voice their concerns. They believed that John's death had been avoidable and approached the local gardaí with a request to find out the truth about what happened on Holy Thursday. They also contacted the *Longford Leader* and voiced their concerns through the newspaper.

The Minister for Justice, John O'Donoghue, overruled my request for an independent inquiry but promised that the facts of the garda investigation would be made public in what would become known as the Culligan Report.

A couple of days after my first public press conference, I telephoned Michael Finucane. Michael, who worked in the well-known solicitors' firm Garrett Sheehan & Co., was aware of the inadvertent role his name had played in the stand-off. He offered me his condolences. He, too, had experienced the death of a beloved member of his family in appalling circumstances, and I knew that his sympathy came from the heart. He suggested I talk to Peter Mullan, the solicitor who would eventually represent me when the campaign for the truth became more demanding and complex. Later, when I met Michael in Dublin, I found him to be very kind and down-to-earth, more than helpful with any advice I needed.

After a number of weeks, I forced myself to watch the television coverage of the stand-off on the internet. I was shocked at how close the media had been allowed to my house. It was agonising to think of John caged behind the broken windows, his mind in turmoil as cameras and microphones recorded the scene. I imagined the loudhailer booming in on him, police in flak jackets with Uzi sub-machine guns and revolvers aimed in his direction. I could feel my anger tightening into a hard knot of determination. With the backing of one of the best legal teams in the country, I hoped to find out why the gardaí had treated a young man suffering from a serious illness like a terrorist or a criminal holding a hostage at gunpoint.

The technical examinations of our old house and the surrounds had been completed. Inevitably, the move home had to be faced and the new house prepared for Rose. When I entered the driveway and saw the broken window, the trampled grass and hedges, the damage to the wall and pillar from the shots John had discharged and the utter desolation of the empty house where the stand-off had been played out, I was filled anew with the horror of it all.

Although the new house was freshly painted and plastered, it was a cold, lonely place to enter. Its modern appearance was a welcome contrast to the old house, which had become increasingly difficult to maintain, and Rose had been looking forward to living in the comfortable, spacious rooms. But the excitement of the move had been replaced by heartbreak and misery. I stayed there on my own for a week, sleeping in the bedroom John had planned to occupy. Rose stayed with her niece, Trisha, on the Coole Road until she felt strong enough to make the journey home. This gave me space to sort out my thoughts and feelings in private.

During the long hours of the stand-off, the new house had been used as a resting place by some of the ERU team. I tried not to think of them moving through the rooms, tried not to hear the echo of their voices. Every time I looked out the living-room window, I could see the deserted house. I longed to wind back the clock until we were children again, with our future shining before us. The feeling of helplessness that had possessed me all the way through the stand-off threatened to consume me. I wanted to hold my beloved brother in my arms and save him from his terrible fate. Two words, 'what if', tortured me, playing out now-impossible scenarios over and over in my mind. What if the mascot goat had never been displayed? What if we hadn't decided to have a new house built? What if John had never inherited Uncle Patsy's gun and become a member of the gun club? What if I'd been at home on Holy Thursday? What if Rose had never left him in the house on his own? What if the phone call to the gardaí seeking help had never been made? On and on it went, a demented chorus in my mind, dredging up all sorts of scenarios that could have averted the tragedy. If only I could walk through the door and see John at the broken window, reaching out his hand to take mine and escape to safety. If only we had been able to get him the help he needed. I felt wracked with grief and, increasingly, anger, unable to begin to imagine how my life would ever return to normal.

Joe Finnegan, a reporter from Shannonside, our local radio station, came to the house to interview me. I broke down in the course of the interview and was unable to continue. He was kind enough to turn off his tape recorder and decided not to turn it back on. He was the first journalist to interview me. He had my story, his emotional scoop, yet out of respect for me and my family, he resisted the urge to exploit my grief. It was an honourable gesture, and I've always respected him for it.

On another occasion, a young woman who worked for an Irish magazine called to our front door and requested an interview. I could tell from her apologetic manner that she obviously didn't want to do her job that day. When I politely told her it wasn't possible, she looked relieved. I guess she was only a rookie and had yet to acquire the tough veneer that journalists need when they have to encroach on a person's personal grief.

Pepper and Trisha helped us move our possessions from one house to the other. The many skills Pepper had acquired from working in the construction industry proved to be a tremendous help to us. Together, we went into Edgeworthstown to choose floor covering. John had planned to do this with Rose; the thought that he should have been the one standing there making decisions came to me as I stood among the rolls of carpets. I almost bent double as a wave of grief swept over me, but I was discovering that even under the most abnormal circumstances, normal activities continue. We made our purchases and helped establish a new home for Rose.

I travelled to Galway with Pepper to bring John's belongings and working tools home. I couldn't bear to show them to Rose and left them in the new attic, where they remain today. She placed John's sporting trophies beside a group of family photographs on the mantelpiece of her living room. Over the years, she'd stored our schoolbooks and many personal items from our childhood and teenage years in the attic. As we explored the crowded storage area, it became an Aladdin's Cave of treasured memories. We had to salvage what we could before the date for demolition.

Three weeks after his death, work began on demolishing the old house. This was in accordance with the agreement we had with the local authority, but we still hadn't managed to remove all our possessions. Moving from one house to another requires energy, decisions on what to keep and what to throw away. We were incapable of making such decisions, exhausted by the effort involved in entering the house where John had spent his final days. The council made no effort to contact us to delay the demolition. We could have protested and insisted on more time to organise ourselves properly, but we walked through those early weeks in a haze of disbelief and shock. In the light of what had happened to John, the demolition of the old house where we had spent so many happy times was just another incomprehensible act. It proved impossible to remove all his personal belongings, and they, too, were buried under the rubble. Other items we'd hoped to salvage were lost, including an old range we intended shifting into the new house. The house was soon razed to the ground.

It was stated afterwards by many legal experts that it should not have been knocked so soon after John's death. Instead, it should have been retained for vital evidence. This 'vital evidence' was now a heap of rubble. It was a harsh memorial, visible every time we walked down our new driveway. In time, the ground was levelled and covered by a smooth green lawn. Some time later, the road where John died was resurfaced. Like his body, buried in the graveyard beyond the hill, all traces of the devastating event were being wiped from Abbeylara.

I stayed with Rose for a number of weeks before returning to Galway. She needed me now more than ever. As a result of all that had occurred, I fell behind in the rent payments for my apartment in Salthill. When I met the landlord to settle the arrears, I was told to vacate the flat due to non-payment of rent. It just another insensitive action at that bleak, lonely time. But there were also so many people who cared. Mass cards and heart-warming messages of sympathy began to arrive from around Ireland and abroad. The number of letters of support astonished us. Many of these letters were from people who suffered from depression or had experience of it, or from their relatives and friends. It's only when something devastating happens that you hear about the terrible tragedies other families have endured. Some letters were anonymous, simply signed, 'A Friend'; others contained small prayer leaflets. To this day, the postman arrives with letters from sympathisers. Many people also travelled from near and far to personally offer their condolences, many of them home from abroad on holiday. I was deeply moved by the outrage people shared at the unnecessary violence of John's death.

Along with the messages of sympathy were letters of a different kind that outlined alleged abuses the writers had suffered at the hands of the gardaí. All asked the same question, which was uppermost in my mind: what would the Culligan Inquiry reveal?

Chief Superintendent Adrian Culligan and his investigation team from Cork commenced their investigation on 21 April 2000. About ten days after John's death, two investigating officers interviewed me in my solicitor's office in Longford town. They asked me questions about my own life before moving on to the subject of John and his depression. Their manner was brusque and business-like. I was asked to give my version of the stand-off. One of the points I made in my statement was that I'd been physically pushed away by Superintendent Byrne when I tried to reach John in the small hours of Holy Thursday.

A few days later, I received a phone call from a local guard who asked me to call into Granard station to answer some questions. This request should have been made through my solicitor, Frank Gearty, but, being a true novice in those early days, I'd no idea of the correct procedure. As a result, I went unaccompanied. One of the investigators was present with a local guard. I was shown my statement and asked if I'd told the whole truth, especially when I claimed to have been pushed by Superintendent Byrne. I repeated that it was true. Rose's version of what happened between her and John before she left the house was also challenged. I was again questioned closely about John's personal life. They claimed he was a gambler and asked if he'd ever given me money when we were living in Galway. I presumed they were referring to a compensation settlement John had received eighteen months previously for a work-related accident. I said I'd no need for John's money – I had my own job, my own independence. But the question was repeated. I found their attitude intimidating. They seemed determined to humiliate my family and made it obvious that they didn't believe me. I was indirectly being called a liar, but there was nothing I could do except wait for the official report to be published.

When John first came to Galway, he supported himself for a number of months until he found work. This used up a certain amount of his compensation package, which had amounted to £18,000. When he returned to Abbeylara, he'd also been unemployed for a few weeks before he started working in Longford. He'd also spent money on clothes and a music centre. I suspect he may also have lent money, possibly when he was in an elated state. But the guards seemed anxious to build up a certain profile of my brother and to prove he'd gambled it away. Like many young men, John sometimes placed a bet in the bookies on a Saturday afternoon, but he was not a gambler in the sense they were insinuating.

When I received a typed copy of my original statement, the point I'd made about being pushed back by the superintendent was missing. I mentioned this to my solicitor and asked to have it reinserted. This request from my solicitor was ignored.

The Culligan team took statements from our neighbours and friends. The community of Abbeylara had many good things to say about John, apart from a handful of people who still believed he was responsible for burning the football-team mascot. John was not perfect and never claimed he was. His mood changes made life difficult sometimes, but he was the main person who suffered. Only someone who has gone through the stark loneliness of depression or the helter-skelter skid of elation can understand the distress and shame it causes the sufferer. But now John's life, as he'd lived it, had become an open book. Every throwaway remark he made, every minor irritation and annoyance, every personality clash or disagreement he'd had with anyone, even the most banal incidents took on a life of their own and were subject to as many interpretations as there were opinions.

During the inquiry, Rose and I had to travel to our solicitor's office in Longford town to attend meetings arranged by the Culligan team. Six weeks after John's death, they told me that his mobile phone records proved he'd tried to phone me from the house. He failed to get a connection. Combined with my deep sadness was an overwhelming relief that he'd turned to me in his time of need. It was a cruel irony that he'd managed to get a clear line to Kevin in Galway but failed to reach me when I was only a short distance up the road from him.

During another one of these meetings, which I attended with Rose, I was handed a small brown envelope and told it contained the personal belongings John had on him the day he died. I couldn't bear to open it in front of the investigators and went with my solicitor to another room. A red cigarette lighter, John's watch and some money were all the envelope contained. Amazingly, his watch was unbroken and displayed the correct time. It has remained in perfect working order since then. It was heartbreaking to look at the small possessions that had been on John's person when he died, and I didn't show them to Rose until we returned to the privacy of our own home later that evening.

We erected a plaque in John's memory beside the spot where he fell and had it engraved with a poem. People often stopped their cars to look at it. Sometimes they called into the house to offer us their condolences or said a prayer by the wall. At other times they just took photographs and drove on.

Two sisters from the village were particularly helpful to us at that time. Anna and Mary Reilly are committee members of the Abbeylara Handball Club and knew John well. Anna decided to contact the Irish Council for Civil Liberties and discuss our situation with them. As a result, I was introduced to Donnacha O'Connell from the ICCL, who became a tremendous support in the years that followed. I wanted to ensure that the truth surrounding John's death was uncovered, but at that early stage of my campaign I was filled with fear at the challenges that lay ahead and was grateful for any practical help I received. As the weeks passed, I discovered a network of people also willing to help uncover the truth, which encouraged me to keep going. On 3 June 2000, before the Culligan Report was released, I once again called for a public inquiry. The Irish Council for Civil Liberties echoed this call and stated that they would be raising this issue with the UN Commission for Human Rights.

My job as a Montessori teacher was kept open for a number of months, but I was unable to take it up again. I'd loved working with children, but they needed my full attention and, under the circumstances, this was impossible. During my student days, I'd worked part-time in a shop and again took up employment there to supplement my income. I stayed in the room in Pepper's house that John had planned to rent. As the publicity grew surrounding the events in Abbeylara, my life was on hold until the Culligan Report was released.

I used to dread looking at the headlines in case Abbeylara was mentioned. It was crushing to look at John's photograph when this happened. He had always called in for a quick chat during the day.

Now that he was no longer there, I kept seeing young men who reminded me of him in some way, the same thick dark hair, his slim build, that big wide grin.

Around 200 people were interviewed as part of the investigation. A five-member FBI team travelled from the USA to advise the Chief Superintendent on international best practice during such situations. Their brief was purely to deal with the police. No other person involved in the stand-off would be questioned. When this news broke, I was flabbergasted. How could the FBI give a clear-cut assessment of how things were handled if they only focused on the garda operation? Surely the people most affected by the shooting should be consulted?

Backed by the Irish Council for Civil Liberties, I issued a statement asking for equal consideration to be given by the FBI to our side of the story. It was ignored, as was a similar call from Deputy Jim Higgins. Garda Commissioner Pat Byrne claimed his decision to call in the FBI was based on a fear that the media would criticise the Culligan Report as a biased one.

In May, a team from *Prime Time*, the RTÉ current-affairs prog-ramme, had travelled to Abbeylara to investigate the sequence of events leading to the shooting. The presenter, Mike Milotte, asked a number of hard questions about the tactics used by the gardaí. They interviewed Kevin Ireland about John's last phone call and asked why it had taken the guards four and a half hours to establish the identity of Michael Finucane. Mike Milottte was able to obtain Michael's mobile-telephone number from a telephone operator in twenty-five seconds, as I had done when I decided to contact him.

The *Prime Time* screening made for emotional viewing, especially when I watched my brother's friends Barney Brady, Bernard Reilly and Ronan Devine describing John as an intelligent and witty young man, a good conversationalist, someone they could rely on. This was the John I knew, but the public were being given a different picture. John was hardly cold in his grave before some papers were publishing

As children, myself and John were inseperable, typical 'Irish twins', with only fourteen months between us in age. More outgoing and confident, John was always very much my 'big brother', and always looked out for me in the schoolyard.

On my communion day with my cousin and godmother Trisha and, below, my family with my cousin Thomas on his confirmation Day. Trisha, Thomas and all my close cousins and relations were a huge part of our lives growing up, and remain so to this day.

Above, another happy family occasion with many of my cousins and our much-loved Aunty Nancy (third from right), Rose's sister. She lived with her family only a few doors away from us, and our two families' lives were closely intertwined through the years.

John (bottom, second from right) with his classmates at an Árd Scoil Phádraig school tour to Paris.

John's passion was handball – he played it at every opportunity and was heavily involved in the restoration of the handball alley at Abbeylara. He was also great with kids and, as a teenager, was often called upon to babysit – above: 'on duty' at my cousin Maura's house.

At home before my debs, with family and friends. John also attended the debs. I'd recently injured my leg playing football and was bravely attempting to look stylish on crutches – which I thought were out of sight when the snap was taken, but which are just in view.

The photo of John, above, was used widely in the media in the aftermath of his killing. Below are his close friends Martin Shelley – 'Pepper' – and Kevin Ireland (right), who were steadfast in their support throughout that difficult time at Abbeylara, and in the bleak aftermath.

The first press conference was held just a week after John was killed. Grief -striken and exhausted, I made a brief statement that we would be seeking an independent public inquiry. Thomas is to the left, Pepper to the right.

At the press conference after the publication of the Barr Report, with solicitor Peter Mullan. Six years on, I faced the media older and more confident. Vindicated at last, Barr's findings would mark a turning-point for myself and Rose. But the simple fact that nothing will ever bring John back to us was never more stark than on that day.

Oifig an Choimisinéara,
An Garda Síochána,
Páirc an Fhionnuisce,
Baile Átha Cliath 8,
Éire.

Office of the Commissioner,
Garda Headquarters,
Phoenix Park,
Dublin 8,
Ireland.

Tel/Teileafón: (01) 666 0000 / 2026

Fax/Facs: (01) 666 2013

Web site: www.garda.ie

E-mail: comstaff@iol.ie

Please quote the following ref. number:
PA 6.01

Date:

PERSONAL & CONFIDENTIAL

Mrs Rose Carthy
Toneymore
Abbeylara
Co. Longford

Dear Mrs Carthy,

I am writing to you on my own behalf as Commissioner of An Garda Síochána and on behalf of all members of An Garda Síochána to express sincere regret at the loss of your son John in Abbeylara on the 20th April 2000.

One of the core functions of An Garda Síochána is the preservation of life, a responsibility we take very seriously and it is therefore most regretful when we experience an outcome where any life is lost. For the loss of John's life and the circumstances which led to it I am truly apologetic.

As you are aware, Mr. Justice Barr has concluded a very in-depth and detailed review of the events at Abbeylara. He has levelled criticism at a number of people, some of whom are within my organisation, and he has outlined many recommendations that in his expressed view may well have altered the outcome.

I can assure you that each and every recommendation and comment contained in that report is being examined by me and my two Deputy Commissioners, and appropriate changes in our procedures will be brought about to ensure that all recommendations are implemented. Indeed many changes have already been made arising from lessons learned from the events surrounding John's death.

We can not change the past but we can certainly endeavour to influence the future and An Garda Síochána, under my control, will do everything possible to ensure that the circumstances which led to the death of John do not arise again.

Once again, I extend my sympathies to you and your daughter Marie and I hope that through the passage of time your pain will ease.

Yours sincerely,

Noel Conroy
Commissioner of An Garda Síochána

27 July 2006

Mission Statement:
To achieve the highest attainable level of Personal Protection, Community Commitment and State Security.

The Garda letter of apology from Noel Conroy, Chief Commissioner, arrived soon after the Barr Report findings, over six years on from John's death (p. 228/9). We were relieved that the Gardaí officially acknowledged their sincere regret over the circumstances that led to John's death, but this apology came too late and did nothing to diminish our loss.

IN LOVING MEMORY OF
JOHN CARTHY
WHO'S LIFE WAS TAKEN TRAGICALLY
ON APRIL 20TH 2000 AGED 27 YEARS
DO NOT STAND BY MY GRAVE AND WEEP
I AM NOT THERE I DO NOT SLEEP
I AM A THOUSAND WINDS THAT BLOW
I AM THE DIAMOND GLINTS UPON THE SNOW
I AM THE SUNLIGHT ON RIPENED GRAIN
I AM THE GENTLE AUTUMN RAIN
I AM THE SOFT STAR THAT SHINES SO BRIGHT
IN ABBEYLARA LATE AT NIGHT

Above, the memorial plaque outside our house at Abbeylara, near the spot where John was shot after he left the house. Below, laying flowers on John's grave.

In Loving Memory Of
JOHN CARTHY Toneymore Abbeylara
Died 12th April 1990
His Son JOHN
Who Died Tragically 20th April 2000 Aged 27 Years
Also His Parents and Brother Terry
In Peace
CARTHY

courtesy of *The Irish Times*

details of his medical background and describing him as a dangerous, armed manic depressive who had left the guards with no option but to shoot. Already the details of the incident in Galway when I'd asked the guards for help was being reported as 'The Arrest of John Carthy in Galway'. That one headline undermined all the good times we'd had since John came to Galway, the fun and laughter we'd shared with our friends.

Through *Prime Time*, I discovered that the ERU had been engaged in two siege-type operations within the past year. Both had yielded very different results to the one that occurred in Abbeylara. One concerned a seven-and-a-half hour stand-off in Kildare involving a recovering drug addict. He demanded medication to help his addiction and surrendered a short time after his request was granted. Another stand-off concerned a wanted man who spoke to the ERU negotiator from the rooftop of a house in Finglas, Dublin. Within a minute of his solicitor arriving, he also surrendered. Why had it been so difficult for John to receive this type of cooperation? Michael Finucane, who appeared on the programme, asked why the gardaí had not immediately contacted the Law Society to check his identity. I can't help wondering if they ever seriously considered John's request. Did they consider the phone call to be the ravings of a mentally disturbed individual and not worth their attention? I couldn't figure what else could explain the lack of action on their part.

On *Prime Time*, Pepper was able to support my claim that I'd been physically pushed and shoved back from the scene. My cousin Ann, who made such determined efforts to persuade the guards to establish a media blackout, spoke about her belief that the intensive publicity had jeopardised the operation. Other concerned friends spoke on John's behalf, including Thomas and the two men from the Abbeylara community who had demanded action and answers, Vincent Quinn and Peter O'Reilly. Another participant was Professor Dermot Walsh from the law department in Limerick University, who challenged the independence of an internal garda investigation. He believed the gardaí would only be able to view the operation through their own eyes and that it would be difficult to deliver a report which would not have a certain bias. This belief would soon be borne out in ways I'd never anticipated.

On Friday, 30 June 2000, the Culligan Report was presented to Justice Minister John O'Donoghue. In case any criminal charges resulted from it, it could not be released until it was studied by the Director of Public Prosecutions. Shortly before its release, leaked details were published in a national newspaper. Reading the article, I felt my heart sinking. It seemed as if the gardaí would be fully exonerated. It found they had acted in an appropriate manner. The only criticism was their failure to provide John with a solicitor. The decision not to allow me contact with John was deemed to be correct procedure. My own belief that the initial approach by the gardaí had been too confrontational was buried under this weight of garda evidence. But I'd no idea just how devastating the findings of the Culligan Report would be for all of us, and particularly for my reputation and self-esteem.

Chapter Eleven

Martin Shelly was brought to the negotiating position by D/Sergeant Jackson. At this time Marie Carthy was anxious to go with Martin Shelly to be nearer her brother. As a result of what D/Sergeant Jackson told me, and my own observation that Marie was under the influence of alcohol, I dissuaded her and physically restrained her from going any nearer the scene . . .

– Extract from Superintendent Byrne's statement to the Culligan Inquiry

Most people will go through their lives without ever experiencing the distress of having their private life torn apart and offered up for public consumption. I received the Culligan Report in the office of Peter Mullan, the solicitor who'd taken my case. I was glad he was with me. Otherwise, I think I would have collapsed as I read page after page of this long-awaited document.

John's medical records were laid bare. Every hospital visit was documented, every pill identified. Words were used with cruel indifference to assassinate his character. He was described as a loner whose only outlet was smoking and drinking. It also stated that he was a gambler. The guards had obviously refused to accept my statement. One particular claim that hurt deeply was that he had overestimated his skill at handball. Remembering the pride with which John had accepted his trophies, I couldn't understand why it was felt necessary to include such a petty comment. Where were the positive remarks made by John's friends and extended family? The subjectivity of a report that was supposed to investigate my brother's death disgusted me.

Kevin came into criticism for taking two hours to make direct contact with the gardaí after John phoned him. They ignored the fact that he'd tried to phone John back and concentrated instead on describing how he'd spent the two hours before calling to the garda station in Galway. No mention was made of the fact that the gardaí had this information almost from the beginning, when it was passed directly on to those in command by the journalist Noeleen Leddy. She had also supplied them with Kevin's mobile number, yet no one considered it worthwhile ringing Kevin to gain further information. It seemed an obvious oversight on the part of trained professionals, yet Kevin was the one held to account, and he was deeply upset by this portrayal.

Superintendent Shelly reported on how he finally managed to identify Michael Finucane. At around 5:30 p.m. on Holy Thursday, he had contacted the office of the Director of Public Prosecutions to check out what criminal charges could be pressed against John when he surrendered. It was during this conversation with a professional officer that he mentioned Michael Finucane's name. The officer was able to tell him who he was and also where he worked, but by then it was too late for the information to be of any use.

In one of Superintendent Shelley's extracts referring to the Wednesday night, he made this comment:

> Some time around 11:40 p.m. I was informed by D/Garda
> Sullivan that John Carthy had requested a solicitor but he

had refused to identify any particular solicitor. I was aware that Inspector Maguire had already made enquiries from Tom Walsh about the possible identity of John Carthy's solicitor and he was informed that John didn't have a solicitor. As he had not identified any particular solicitor it was not possible to identify who he was talking about.

I knew I'd given that information to the gardaí when I was being questioned about John on the Ballywillian side of our house. Thomas had also verified this fact. He was standing outside with Superintendent Shelly when he leaned into the jeep where I was being interviewed by Detective Garda Sullivan and asked the name of our solicitor.

'Gearty's,' I'd replied, mentioning the name of the Longford firm that had always looked after our family's affairs.

But in the Culligan Report, Superintendent Shelly was stating that he'd never received such information. Even if what he said was true, there had been plenty of time throughout Holy Thursday to check those details with John's immediate family. We'd been anxious to pass on any information that could bring an end to the stand-off. The gardaí were trained to obtain information from people in emergency situations, yet they failed to do so, leaving us to cope as best we could during the most devastating crisis of our lives.

When my name was mentioned, it was done brutally. I was accused of being 'under the influence of alcohol' on the night the stand-off began. At first, I couldn't take in what I was reading. I kept going back over this comment line by line, made by Superintendent Byrne, trying to understand how he could have come to this conclusion.

Throughout Wednesday, I'd been working in Galway. It was seven in the evening when my employer gave me a lift to my apartment. A statement was never taken from her. I arrived home only minutes before I received the phone call from Ann. Less than thirty minutes later, the squad car had collected me. A garda escort brought me to Abbeylara. How could I have arrived on the scene in a state of intoxication, unless I was drinking either during working hours or in the garda car on the journey to Abbeylara? The only other possibility was that I'd managed to become drunk between the time I arrived in Abbeylara and returned to the scene some hours later. One hot whiskey, kindly prepared for us by Mrs Devine when we went to her house after we'd been standing around Ballywillian in the cold, was the sole extent of the alcohol I drank that night.

The idea was preposterous, but there it was in black and white. My distress over what was happening, my annoyance with the guards for not allowing me to speak to John and my very justified fear for his safety and mental state, not to mention the safety of those surrounding him, had been seen as the reaction of a hysterical woman with too much drink on her.

There was nothing I could do to prevent this information from going out into the public domain. Yet, as I continued reading other extracts that mirrored what Superintendent Byrne had stated, there was no doubt in my mind that a serious allegation had been made against me.

30.3. *The evidence of D/Sergeant Jackson is that Marie was very distressed, she appeared to have drink taken and it was the members' opinion that if she was left to the Negotiation Point she might become more agitated, because of her condition and behaviour. It was the D/Sergeant's concern that she may unwittingly inflame the situation and might compromise her own safety and that of others. It is also the evidence of the Scene Commander that Marie was under the influence of drink, he had to dissuade and physically restrain her. After this she composed herself and sat with Garda personnel in the Command vehicle, while Shelly was at the Negotiation Point.*

30.4. There is also evidence from D/Garda Campbell that Marie was under the influence of alcohol and insisted on going to speak to her brother.

30.5. It is interesting to note that she made no reference of being restrained in her own statement to the investigation.

This was outrageous. I'd made that very point in my original statement, but it had been erased. Now, coldly and deliberately, it was being used against me. Utterly deflated, I began to cry. I was still in a state of shock over John's death, and now I had to deal with the arrogance and authority of a police force which was determined to discredit me. Was this because I'd dared to ask questions, to speak out and voice my anger?

It was stated in the report that cigarettes were not given to John because of safety concerns and also because he refused to cooperate with his negotiator:

The question of cigarettes was seen by the Negotiator as an area to build trust between himself and Carthy. It was not the case of refusing to give them. The Negotiator had cigarettes at the Negotiation Point on the morning of Thursday, 20th April, 2000 but due to Carthy's non co-operation safe delivery was not achieved. The course followed by the Negotiator in relation to the cigarettes is a well established procedure in crisis negotiation.

However, another section read:

In a statement of Thomas Walsh to Mr Gearty, solicitor, Longford, Walsh states having left the Negotiation Point, upset and frustrated, after failed negotiations, he then moved to the outer cordon and in answer to a request by him to get cigarettes for Carthy, a Garda is alleged to have stated, 'No, he is acting the bollox, he is not getting his own

way now.' This investigation is satisfied that this loose
remark is not attributed to any member who had a direct
function in the management of this scene.

If that was the case, I had only one question to ask – what was a guard
or civilian who had no direct function in the stand-off doing at the
scene of an armed and dangerous operation? The extent of this
danger was emphasised in the final stages of the report:

Finally, it is felt that the tragic loss of life in this case is most
regrettable and has been very traumatic for the Carthy
family. However, bearing in mind the 25-hour siege and the
activities engaged in by John Carthy, which placed Gardaí
and civilians at serious risk to life, the circumstances then
prevailing required an effective and immediate response. It
must be stated that the Gardaí present at the time of the
fatal shooting showed extreme courage and perseverance in
allowing Carthy every opportunity to put the weapon down
and have the matter resolved peacefully. However, Carthy
failed to respond to all exhortations and the members were
left with no alternative but to discharge their weapons.
They acted entirely within the Garda Síochána Regulations
and also within the law of the State.

The five-member team from the FBI concluded in their report that the
main problem with the garda operation was that they did not shoot
John soon enough. They allowed him to walk undeterred beyond the
wall towards the outer perimeter, which was manned in part by
unarmed garda officers.

How could the FBI analyse what had happened in Abbeylara?
They worked to a different ethos. I'd read about their high-profile
operations. In Waco, Texas they'd ended a siege with tanks and
chemical weapons. In the fire that followed, over sixty men, women

104

and children perished. What on earth were they doing adding their voice to this unjust and biased report, which reduced my reputation and John's to tatters?

Chief Superintendent Adrian Culligan stated that it was not his intention, nor that of the force, to hurt my family or cause us further upset. But, he added, it was not his fault if John had certain problems. It was his duty to highlight them. But why did he not also have a duty to highlight all the positive statements that had been made by the community of Abbeylara to the investigators? Surely it was his responsibility to give a balanced view of my brother instead of this one-sided version that exonerated the gardaí from any blame and diminished John's personality, stripping it of any humanity other than that of a dangerous manic depressive.

The community of Abbeylara was furious over these highly subjective findings. Peter O'Reilly, in particular, was appalled. He'd been active in encouraging the local people to cooperate with the investigators, and this was the result. After the selective leaks appeared in the media, he'd written a furious letter to the Garda Commissioner, complaining about the fact that a deliberate attempt was being made to destroy John's reputation. The *Longford Leader* was also highly critical of the findings, but the Culligan Report was done and dusted. It was there for anyone to read. Those who were not inclined to read such a long report could read the more titillating details in the daily tabloids.

In an effort to cope, I read books about the grieving process and its seven stages: shock or disbelief, denial, bargaining, guilt, anger, depression and, finally, acceptance and hope. I began to imagine that there might be an end to this as I moved through the various stages, but I quickly discovered that nothing could be further from the truth. My emotions were all over the place. Sometimes it seemed like I was going through many of the stages at the same time. The only one that remained outside my understanding was acceptance.

I seemed to be in a permanent state of shock, which was only intensified after the release of the Culligan Report. As for disbelief, it was all-consuming. I kept thinking it had to be a dream, one of those terrifying, vivid nightmares that leave you flooded with relief when you awaken. Yet I was constantly being forced to confront the reality, especially when I opened the morning papers or turned on the television. The accusation that I was drunk at the scene had been immediately seized on by the media. Seeing my name in print, often accompanied by a photograph, was horrendous. Holy Thursday was an appropriate day for this tragedy to occur – I felt as if I'd been crucified in public. The gossip continued. People I met regularly mentioned the drink allegation, asking if there was any truth behind it. Others took it for granted that what they read had to be true. I fast learned that mud sticks, and I'm sure there are many people who still believe that I was drunk during my brother's ordeal.

I don't remember going through the bargaining stage of grief. I imagine it takes place during a long illness, where there is time to haggle with God about the worth of a life. If a death is sudden and shocking, there is not time to make such demands. Even the word 'bargaining' had painful connotations, bringing to mind the cigarettes the guards used as a bargaining tool when John was so desperate for help

My sleep was filled with nightmares. John was always alive in my dreams, yet somehow, even in my deepest sleep, I knew something was wrong. I'd awaken to an instant realisation that he was gone for ever. There was denial also, instants of forgetfulness when I would imagine I'd hear him at the door and turn, expecting to see him arriving in. I'd hear a car passing and automatically stare out the window. Whenever my phone rang, I'd think for a few seconds that he was calling me and sometimes found myself lifting my phone to ring him.

The most intense feeling was loss. I felt as if part of me was missing and had no idea how I would ever find it again. Then there was the guilt, the belief that I should have done more, forced my way through the cordon, shouted down the gardaí. Why had I given in so easily to their instructions, allowed them to browbeat me out of the way?

I'd loved John dearly, yet at times his illness was difficult to handle. I kept thinking of instances when I could have been more understanding, forgetting the many times I'd helped him in every possible way. As for anger, I had so many targets, I didn't know where to direct it. I seriously believed I'd be stuck permanently in that particular stage. Initially, I felt anger towards John for not phoning me, but that disappeared after I was told about his efforts to contact me. I railed at God, demanded to know where He'd been throughout my brother's ordeal. I'd been reared as a Catholic, taught to believe there was a divine meaning to everything, but I could find none here.

One day, shortly after his death, when we were still going through his possessions, the bishop of the diocese, Colm O'Reilly, and our then local priest, Fr Fitzpatrick, called to visit us. It was a very supportive gesture at such a difficult time in our lives. I wanted to ask them to explain God's meaning in such a meaningless tragedy, but I kept silent, knowing I'd be unable to accept any explanation about mysterious ways and acceptance of God's will.

I read about acceptance and wondered if I would ever achieve it. Rose was coping as best she could, but it was heartbreaking to watch her becoming frail from the constant stress, crying over newspaper features. She'd visit Nancy, who would comfort her and try to take her mind off things for a short while. My cousins watched out for her when I wasn't at home, but I could see that she was just drifting from day to day. I felt so helpless, knowing she was keeping up a brave face in front of me. She's a quiet person by nature and didn't want to talk about her grief in case she upset me. I felt the same way about her. We both needed to express our feelings, but John's death and the consequences that followed seemed too enormous to be expressed through words.

Since the tragedy, there had been no official communication from the Minister for Justice John O'Donoghue or his department. As the date for the inquest drew nearer, I was filled with a mix of dread and anticipation. Although the power and scope of the inquest would be limited, and the jury wasn't expected to attribute blame or exonerate anyone, I still hoped it would lead the way towards a deeper understanding of how the stand-off was conducted. Unlike the Culligan investigation, the information would be presented openly, and witnesses would have to answer questions.

Up to a week beforehand, neither Rose nor myself had been officially invited to attend the Coroner's Court, although some of the neighbours were asked to be present. Nor did we know if the members of the ERU who fired the fatal shots would take the stand. On the opening day, the inquest was adjourned for six weeks. Our legal team believed they needed more time to examine statements and depositions.

As they worked towards this new date, I tried to pull myself together after the intensive publicity following the Culligan Report. An opportunity came in September, when I was asked to speak at the Irish Council for Civil Liberties annual meeting. An extract from my speech was published in their newsletter:

John Carthy – A Personal Memory

John Carthy was a great brother to have. He was always there when I needed him. He did everything he possibly could for both my mother and I, even more so when my father died ten years ago. John was a very intelligent person, very witty, trustworthy, easy-going, gentle and hard-working. While working in Galway he often worked seven days a week.

John had a keen interest in handball; he helped rebuild the old handball alley in Abbeylara. There he took part in tournaments where he won several trophies. He enjoyed game shooting, fishing and playing pool. Everywhere John went he made very good friends and was well respected by all of them. He was the type of person everyone would take time out to listen and talk to.

Like so many people worldwide John suffered from depression, but with his intelligence, good family and friends had long learned to cope with it. John never hurt anyone in his life and was not capable of hurting himself or anyone else.

Finally, life without John will never be the same because he was always there. It is appalling how his life was cut so short when he had so many things going for him. His right to life was taken so suddenly from him.

I hoped this simple tribute to John would help in some small way to restore his tarnished reputation. I'd addressed an audience who was willing to look beyond the image of a manic-depressive so cruelly outlined in the Culligan Report and sections of the media.

Chapter Twelve

Professor Harbison, the State Pathologist, has reported and the verdict of the inquest jury has found that the cause of death was a left haemothorax due to lacerations of the heart and left lung due to a bullet wound to the chest and upper abdomen. Professor Harbison has reported that the bullet wound which he described as the fatal shot had a different trajectory to the other bullets. Its entry was nine inches above the entry to what is believed to have been the third bullet, and was just to the right of the midline, over his spine and the angle of the trajectory was upwards and to the left rather than down. The exit in the left nipple area was approximately nine and a half inches above the entry.
   – Barr Tribunal report

On 9 October, the inquest began in the Longford Coroner's Court. By a cruel twist of fate, the delay in holding John's inquest meant that it opened on the day he would have celebrated his twenty-eighth birthday. The story of the stand-off at Abbeylara had spread beyond Ireland, and a gathering of international journalists as well as the Irish media were present. It was harrowing to walk through the camera crews lining the footpath. I wanted to cover my face, but I mustered what courage I could and held my head high as I passed them by. The uniformed guards went in the front entrance, but the ERU members chose a more discreet entrance, reluctant to have their identities revealed. I wondered why there was so much concern about the anonymity of the ERU officers when the Garda Press Office had allowed journalists and camera crews so close to the scene on Holy Thursday. The image of the guards crouched behind our gate pillar had become synonymous with the final day of John's life.

A jury was sworn in, and the four-day ordeal began. Three members of the gardaí repeated the accusation that I was intoxicated on the night of the siege. When the time came to read my statement, I broke down. The Culligan Report had undone all my efforts to keep going. I pulled myself together and finished my statement, but it sounded formal and unemotional, hollow. I wanted to tell them how I really felt, to let everyone hear the true extent of my anger. Thomas told of his efforts to speak to John and how, in his opinion, the constant dialogue by the gardaí had 'been driving John mad'. Kevin gave evidence that John told him he had no intention of shooting anybody. Apart from asking for a solicitor, John had said a number of other things to him on the phone. He believed that 'sixty cowardly guards' were surrounding him. He'd no intention of harming himself or anyone else, but his bravado warning to Kevin, 'watch this space', was the only part of their conversation that the gardaí seemed to regard with any significance.

Rose was too upset to read her statement aloud. On the fourth day, Ann and I escorted her into the packed courtroom. She was shaking as I brought her to the witness box. She was unable to hold back her tears, and her statement was read aloud by our senior counsel, Patrick Gageby. In the hushed courtroom, I held her hand, barely able to contain my own emotion. To add to her distress, John's shotgun was brought into the courtroom as part of the evidence. To this day, I still can't believe that someone didn't have the sensitivity to take away the gun, which was clearly within her sight while she was in the witness chair.

Upsetting as it was, the inquest gave us a disturbing insight into the activities of the gardaí after John left the house. Patrick Gageby cast doubt on the garda claim that John was still standing after the third shot was fired, going into a detailed analysis of where Detective Garda Aidan McCabe was positioned when he began to fire. From the trajectory of the fourth bullet through John's body, it appeared that he was already falling when it hit him. Our barrister argued that he was already fatally wounded at that stage and was falling forward as a result of the third shot. In effect, this meant that the fourth shot should not have been fired. This was disputed by the gardaí, who had always claimed he'd continued moving with three bullets inside him.

I wanted to cover my ears. First, the Culligan Report, and now this formal dissection of the events of John's killing. While legal minds argued over the trajectory of bullets, all I could imagine was shattered bone and flesh, a heart no longer beating. But I forced myself to listen and absorb the information. It was the least I could do for John.

Some of the jury looked confused by the mass of conflicting technical evidence. They were told by the County Coroner Mr Gerry McDonagh that they had the option of three verdicts. They could decide John died by misadventure; they could conclude an open verdict – which could lead the way to a public enquiry; or, finally, they could conclude that he'd died from injuries he'd received after being shot. The jury opted for the latter choice. It was less complicated to state the self-evident fact that John had died from gunshot wounds.

'Having listened to all the evidence presented to us relating to the tragic death of John Carthy, we are satisfied the identity was John Carthy and that he was shot by gardaí at Toneymore, Abbeylara on 20 April 2000.' They then extended their sympathy to his relations and friends and hoped John would rest in peace.

How could he rest in peace? How could any of us rest peacefully while so many questions remained unanswered? Despite a plea from our barrister that they consider several recommendations on how such situations could be handled in the future, the jury made no effort to do so. Some weeks after the inquest, I met one of the jurors and he told me that he'd found it impossible to grasp the more complex details, and this had affected the decision he made.

The inquest was a tough and disappointing four days. With the help of family, friends and an excellent legal team, we got through it. As I left the courtroom, I knew there was a long road ahead. A full public inquiry which allowed a proper cross-examination of witnesses and an independent conclusion was now the only way to go.

The week ended with a *Late Late Show* appearance. Shortly after John's death, I'd been asked to go on the show but refused. I didn't feel up to the task and had agreed to go on when the show returned from its summer break. The date was set for Friday, 13 October 2000.

The idea of going live on air was frightening. Some members of my extended family still felt it was too soon to appear on such a high-profile programme, but I knew I needed to take the opportunity to tell the viewers what John was really like and redeem my own damaged reputation.

Pepper, Thomas, Kevin and two other cousins, Maura and Trisha, came with me for moral support. Once they arrived, they were brought to the audience and I was taken to make-up. I watched part of the show in the green room, envying the other guests who looked so composed and confident. I met the actress Barbara Windsor and singer Daniel O'Donnell before my turn came to be interviewed. They assured me there was no need to be nervous. Little did they know that I was the kind of person whose knees knocked together even doing a reading in my local church.

By the time I was called, I was convinced I'd be unable to open my mouth to answer Pat Kenny's questions. The presenter kindly came backstage to meet me before I went on. His calm, professional approach helped quell my nerves. He assured me I would be fine and asked if I'd like to walk on live. Afraid my legs would give way, I declined. While Daniel O'Donnell was on stage singing, I settled myself into the hot seat. Then, suddenly, I was on air. Much to my amazement, all my nerves disappeared. I could see my cousins and John's friends seated in the audience. I felt John's presence very close to me. I knew that if our positions had been reversed, he, too, would be sitting in the same seat, telling my story.

Pat was very sensitive in his questioning. I was proud of myself that night. I'd crossed a certain barrier and was able to tell my story to the nation without falling apart. This helped, somewhat, to ease the hurt of the Culligan Report. During my interview, Pat walked down to the audience and spoke briefly to Thomas, Kevin and Pepper. They weren't expecting this to happen, but they were well able to put their points of view across.

We stayed overnight in Dublin. The next day, I was astonished at the number of people who recognised me when I was walking through the city. I was learning quickly about the power of the media, but I wondered when I returned home that night if I was losing my own identity. From now on, would I only be recognised as the sister of John Carthy? Not that I cared – it was a small price to pay for the truth.

The fall-out from the Culligan Report continued. Nothing about our personal lives remained private. I received anonymous letters demanding that I stop calling for a public inquiry. I was to leave the guards alone. This feeling of being under observation was unnerving, and I'm not sure how I would have coped but for my friends, who were always there when I needed them. When I first moved to Galway and was studying to be a Montessori teacher, I did some babysitting for a couple, James and Aine Walsh, who had two wonderful children, James and Christina. They had met John during his time in Galway and were very supportive of me when I tried to settle back in. Pepper and Kevin worked nearby and regularly called into the shop to check on me. Another friend, Siobhan Judge, encouraged me with media interviews. 'Go for it,' she'd say. 'Don't be nervous. There's nothing to it. You'll fly through it.' After I'd complete one, she'd admit, 'My God, Marie, I don't know how you did it. I'd have died on the spot!'

To have so many friends willing to help and to make me laugh made my days more bearable. Nonetheless, socialising with them was becoming increasingly difficult. Everyone I met seemed to know what had happened. Even a quiet night out with a few friends would be interrupted with people enquiring about myself and Rose. Strangers who recognised me from the television reports came over to introduce themselves. This exposure was difficult to handle so soon after the tragedy.

Some months after John's death, when I returned home for a weekend, I met with friends in the Park House Hotel in Edgeworthstown. In the course of the evening, one of my friends introduced me to a man called Patrick. When he heard my name, he didn't blink or express surprise or, as in some cases, fall silent with embarrassment. He simply sat down beside me and started chatting about ordinary things. I soon discovered that he had just returned from an overseas work trip and knew nothing about my circumstances. To be able to chat to someone without reference to our tragedy was a great release, and our friends made no effort to bring John's name into the conversation.

The following day, Patrick phoned me to see if I'd returned home safely. We chatted for a while. Again, it was a normal conversation, and I did nothing to enlighten him about my identity. Patrick's work involved a lot of international travelling, his trips often lasting for a number of weeks. Shortly after we met, I changed my mobile-phone number. The media were constantly ringing, and I needed some protection from the publicity. We lost contact, but that brief encounter had been a relief from the constant presence of grief and emotional turmoil.

I continued working in the shop in Galway. Often there were untruths or distortions printed in the newspapers about myself or

John. I was unable to sleep at night when I knew something was going to make the papers the next day. The embarrassment of having to sell these newspapers to our regular customers is something I'll never forget. I'd watch as customers picked up the paper and averted their eyes. Some would smile sympathetically or pass some remark about the media. I felt as if I was grieving in a goldfish bowl with nowhere to hide my emotions. I considered giving up the job, but getting ready for work each morning gave my day a structure, and I refused to allow the unwelcome publicity to isolate me even more.

Armed with the Culligan Report and the inquest findings, *Prime Time,* again presented by Mike Milotte, returned to Abbeylara to do a follow-up programme. Many people in the parish were offended by the Culligan Report and felt that their opinions had been totally ignored or misrepresented. Whereas *The Late Late Show* had given space for my friends and I to defend John's reputation, *Prime Time* engaged in another in-depth investigation. The programme questioned whether the decision to bring in the ERU was an overreaction to a situation that could have been resolved in a much less heavy-handed fashion. The events surrounding the twenty-five-hour stand-off and the subsequent gathering of information by the garda team were also examined.

Local people such as Peter O'Reilly and Vincent Quinn were given an opportunity to express their surprise and anger at the Culligan Report which, they believed, had ignored their opinions and concerns. Professor Dermot Walsh, one of Ireland's experts on police procedure, also added his voice to the growing unease as to how the report had been compiled.

'The statements should have first come from those who fired the first shot,' explained Professor Walsh. 'They started off first of all by taking statements from the local gardaí. Then they took statements from the armed detectives. Then statements were taken from the ERU members who didn't fire the shots. Then they took statements from the ERU members who did fire the shots. Ultimately, they took statements from the scene commanders. The statement should have come first of all from those who had fired the shots. They're the most critical players in this operation, and it was crucially important that statements were taken from them at the earliest opportunity. It's equally important that statements are taken from all other players involved in such an operation in a manner and at a time that limits the opportunity for collusion, limits the opportunity for comparing stories and, ultimately, ensures that the accounts that ensue are as accurate as they possibly can be.'

But, as *Prime Time* outlined, the officer who fired the first shot made his statement three weeks after the event. The officer who fired the fatal shot wasn't interviewed until four and a half weeks later. The scene commanders made their statements after six weeks.

My cousin Maura spoke for all of us when she asked why no serious effort was made at the earliest opportunity to seek psychiatric advice instead of leaving it until it was too late to be of any use. It was twelve hours after the ERU arrived and sixteen hours after the siege started before information about Dr Shanley was obtained. Assistant Commissioner Hickey, who had made the decision to call in the ERU, had known about John's mental condition by seven o'clock on the Wednesday evening, but the scene commander, Superintendent Shelly, claimed he wasn't aware of this fact until an hour later. When Detective Sergeant Jackson, the negotiator, arrived on the scene, he requested a full medical background. There was no evidence he was given this information. Dr Cullen phoned Granard station at 11:00 p.m. to check how the situation with John was developing. No one asked for his advice or assistance at that time. They waited until four in the morning before a garda officer was sent to his house for information. Dr Cullen, although he knew John's medical background, was not a psychiatrist and was unable to provide the specialist knowledge needed to deal with this serious manifestation of his illness.

Both Thomas and I had an opportunity to explain how we had

given the guards our family solicitor's name on the Wednesday night. Thomas also stated that one of the guards who entered our driveway in the early stages of the siege told him that John had not shot in their direction. They could have been a target if he had attempted to do so, but instead he deliberately aimed at the police car. As his gun was used for hunting and was only loaded with birdshot, it did minimal damage to the wing of the car.

Towards the end of the programme, computerised graphics were used to show how John had exited the house and the sequence of events that followed. It was harrowing to watch this virtual final journey and see how he had been brought down. But the Culligan Report had brought him down a second time when they callously smeared his reputation in an effort to protect their own.

'If I was a member of John's family or a friend I'd be appalled by the manner in which he was deconstructed and demeaned in that report,' said Donnacha O'Connell from the Irish Council for Civil Liberties. 'Every detail of the medication he ever took, every conversation, every second-hand account of every conversation he ever had, every negative impression of a person that could be given was magnified in a report that was an appalling insult to his memory.'

Chapter Thirteen

SUB-COMMITTEE ON ABBEYLARA INCIDENT ANNOUNCES DETAILS OF PARLIAMENTARY INQUIRY

The Chairman of the sub-Committee on the Abbeylara Incident, Mr Seán Ardagh TD, today announced details of the Parliamentary Inquiry into the Abbeylara Incident which will commence on Tuesday 24 April 2001.

The Inquiry will be held over a three week period and will hear evidence from the Carthy family and friends, members of An Garda Síochána, Medical Personnel and Firearms experts.

In addition, the sub-Committee, as part of its Inquiry will visit Abbeylara on Wednesday 25 April 2001.

Speaking at a briefing this afternoon, the Chairman of the sub-Committee, Mr Seán Ardagh TD said that it was incumbent on this particular Inquiry to bring a sensitivity and reverence to the manner in which the tragic events at Abbeylara were to be investigated.

'Of course we are mindful that fair and just procedures are an essential and defining aspect of how we will conduct our proceedings over the next few weeks. To act otherwise than uphold our Terms of Reference would be to imperil the very democratic procedures that brought this inquiry into being and

*to render a great disservice to all parties concerned, whose
wish in each case is that all the circumstances of this tragic
event are made manifest.'*
– *Press release, 18 April 2001*

The year turned full circle. We crowded into our local church to
attend John's first anniversary mass. His grave was covered with fresh
flowers. Twelve months had made a big difference to our
surroundings. All evidence of the dramatic stand-off was gone. The
old gatepost, shown so often in the filming of the siege, had been
plastered and painted, and Rose's house now had a lived-in look. In
John's room, the scent of lavender filled the air, but the overall feeling
of emptiness, of waiting for someone, always struck me as soon as I
entered. There was still no chance to come to terms with his death or
cope in private with my grief. I was always reaching outwards towards
the next hurdle, coping with the next interview, dreading what the
next media report would claim.

The former Taoiseach Albert Reynolds was aware that there was a
growing concern in the community about the events surrounding the
stand-off and how it had been reported in the Culligan Report. Like
many people, he'd initially believed that the report and the
subsequent inquest would reveal the truth, but when this didn't
materialise, he contacted Taoiseach Bertie Ahern and called for a
sworn independent inquiry. Mr Reynolds also came to visit us in
Abbeylara and listened to our concerns. I sensed that this was a man
who genuinely felt we'd been let down by our police force and that his
voice would be a powerful addition to our campaign.

The Government, while still refusing us a public inquiry,
announced the establishment of an Oireachtas seven-member sub-
committee to investigate the shooting. This would be chaired by
Fianna Fáil TD Sean Ardagh. The other FF members were TDs
Marian McGennis, Michael Moynihan and Senator Denis Donovan.

Fine Gael was represented by TDs Alan Shatter and Monica Barnes, and TD Brendan Howlin was the Labour Party representative.

On 25 April 2001, they came to Abbeylara. According to Sean Ardagh, they wanted to see the location of the siege for themselves rather than relying on maps. They were anxious to keep their inspection private, so instead of gathering at St Bernard's Church, where the media were waiting, they arrived at our house by the Ballywillian road at around 11:40 a.m. To help them do their work, Thomas had marked out the site where our cottage once stood with stakes and string. Pieces of paper showing the position of the door and windows fluttered in the breeze. It was a grey, sullen day, but a silent one, no loudspeakers, no bullets echoing. I always made strenuous efforts to protect Rose from the worst aspects of the publicity surrounding John's death, but I had been in Dublin for the formal opening of the investigation and wasn't in Abbeylara when they arrived. She walked home from the village where she had been shopping and passed the television cameras outside her house. Bunches of flowers lay on the grass at the spot where her son died, placed there by neighbours, family and friends for his first anniversary. She found it incomprehensible that a group of politicians were in Abbeylara to investigate her son's death. Her quiet existence had been shattered by all that had happened, and her home was her refuge. She closed the front door on the press and the politicians. No matter what they recorded or discovered, nothing would bring her son back to her.

Our hopes that this would be a clear-cut investigation had been dashed on the opening day. I sat in Kildare House, intimidated by the formal surroundings and with no idea what to expect. Full legal representation had been granted to us, but having never attended anything like this in my life, I was relieved to have Thomas and Pepper beside me. Together, we could make sense of what was happening.

The key issues to be considered over the next three weeks included the events surrounding John's shooting, the state of his health or illness, the issue of firearms and the role of the gardaí. The other issues concerned the function of the role of the coroner in the inquest, the role of the gardaí and the Department of Justice and their relationship. These headings were encouraging and promised a thorough investigation, yet from the beginning, the tension between the gardaí and the sub-committee was obvious.

Mr John Rogers, speaking on behalf of the gardaí, was the first to sound the death knell of the investigation when he addressed the chairman with these words: 'Sir, you are engaged on the most dangerous and treacherous of a journey across the most choppy waters because of this.' He added that the gardaí – already cleared by a separate investigation – could not be cross-examined again.

I've no idea how the sub-committee felt about this threat, but my heart sank as soon as I heard it. My experience with the Culligan Report had left me in no doubt about the gardaí's ability to protect themselves. Their legal team then made a submission claiming it would be dangerous and unfair for a political committee to investigate the events surrounding John's shooting. This submission was rejected by the Chairman Sean Ardagh, who said that despite the findings in the Culligan Report, his committee could legitimately investigate the facts. He added that there was no finality to the Culligan Report findings simply because Garda Commissioner Pat Byrne had accepted all it contained.

For the short duration of the enquiry, John Rogers regularly objected to questions from committee members and claimed they were implying that some gardaí were guilty of wrongdoing. It was revealed that two members of the ERU had gone back to the scene several days after the siege without the knowledge of Chief Superintendent Adrian Culligan, who subsequently investigated the shooting. Yet Thomas had seen them on the site, had spoken briefly to them and mentioned this encounter to the Culligan investigative team. John Rogers objected to the ERU officers being questioned about their decision to revisit the scene and asked that the inquiry be stopped so that the evidence from those at the scene be taken first. True facts rather than hearsay must be established, he demanded. All I wanted to know was why the investigation team had used the most subjective hearsay when they interviewed people about my brother's character. I also discovered that the bullets fired at John were never recovered, despite an exhaustive search. The fact that these bullets could still be hidden somewhere along the grassy verges on the hedgerows or in the fields where we used to play filled me with horror.

Deputy Sean Ardagh accused Mr Rogers of raising nitty-gritty legal issues and trying to put a spanner in the works of the investigation. Despite his robust reaction, my initial instincts proved to be correct. After sitting for only two days – during which time Garda Commissioner Pat Byrne defended his force's decision to call in the ERU and Chief Superintendent Adrian Culligan told the committee that it would be wrong to indicate that a person who was shot would automatically fall down, even if they were shot four times – the investigation was adjourned for a month.

We weren't the only ones angered and frustrated by this delay. Labour TD Brendan Howlin claimed that there was a concerted effort to frustrate the work of the Oireachtas sub-committee. I stood on the steps of Kildare House and told journalists that my family was angry and frustrated by what was happening to this new inquiry. Why had the ERU officers not expressed these concerns before the inquiry began? I was beginning to sound like a broken record as I called again for an independent inquiry. 'There is a public perception that gardaí are unwilling to answer questions about what happened to John,' I concluded. 'We share that perception.'

I tried to remain composed, but facing the media was always daunting. I had developed a hearty respect for people who could speak effortlessly in front of a microphone and realised that achieving this effortless flow was a lot harder than it looked. Yet, each time I was forced to do so, it became a little easier, especially when I believed utterly in what I was saying.

The sub-committee was unwilling to admit they'd hit a brick wall. Sean Ardagh announced that this was only a short adjournment and they would be back in action within a month. The weeks passed. Regular media reports revealed that the ERU members involved in the siege wanted to be exempted from giving evidence in public. Revealing their identity could compromise their performance in the future, their legal representative claimed. The committee were surprised by this development. Before the investigation had begun, the chief state solicitor had advised them that the ERU officers were prepared to be identified by name and to give evidence. The arguments dragged on. The ERU could be provided with screens, if necessary. Minister O'Donoghue had no objections to the Oireachtas sub-committee completing its investigation as long as there were no cameras when certain gardaí and members of the ERU were giving evidence. 'There is a need in the national interest to protect the identity of those involved,' he stated. I thought back again to the hyped media exposure on the Toneymore Road and wondered how exactly the images broadcast and printed fit in with what was being said now.

Despite the chairman's optimism that the inquiry would continue, it was obvious when the month was up that the Oireachtas sub-committee would be unable to reconvene until its position was legally challenged. The garda legal teams had decided to go to the High Court to seek a judicial inquiry. Thirty-six gardaí, including nine members of the ERU, made the challenge. They stated that TDs and senators weren't the appropriate people to carry out this type of adjudication. The hearing would allow the High Court to decide if the sub-committee had the right to question rank-and-file gardaí about their actions during the stand-off rather than to concentrate on putting questions to senior officers about policy decisions. John Rogers believed his clients should have a public inquiry under the tribunals of inquiry legislation. At least we were agreed on something.

There would be no further sittings while the legal proceedings were ongoing. The High-Court hearing would be held in July. Backed by the other members of the sub-committee, Fine Gael deputy Alan Shatter personally took on the gardaí in their High Court case, but the hearing was adjourned until October, and we had to wait until November to hear the results. Regardless of who won, we knew the decision would be appealed to the Supreme Court. It was impossible to concentrate on anything. My mind was completely preoccupied with the Oireachtas inquiry and the threat to its continuation.

Eventually, no longer able to handle the exposure, I stopped working in the shop. I loved living in Galway, but too many memories of happier times and my constant worry about Rose made it impossible to settle back there. I returned to Abbeylara, but even in the village, among our small community, I was embarrassed going out. I knew there were differing opinions over how the garda operation had been handled. The majority of people were extremely kind to me, but it was only human nature to talk about the publicity following the Culligan Report. How to distinguish fact from fantasy wasn't easy when there was a constant barrage of publicity coming from all angles, some good, some negative, some so far removed from the truth that I could hardly recognise myself or John any more.

The thirty-six gardaí, including the nine members of the ERU, won their High Court challenge. The case lasted for nineteen days and the judgment found that such inquiries did not have the power to make findings of fact or expressions of opinion adverse to the good name or reputation of citizens. I was at home in Abbeylara with Rose when our solicitor, Peter Mullan, rang with the news. Alan Shatter claimed that the consequences of the judgment created a major constitutional crisis for the Oireachtas. If the committee's appeal to the Supreme Court was unsuccessful, there should be a referendum on the issue.

Apart from the personal and emotional distress Rose and I were feeling about this long-drawn-out situation, there was a sense of disbelief when I heard words like 'constitutional crisis' and 'referendum'. Like John's siege, we were being carried along on a wave that had moved widely outside our control. All we wanted was the truth and some kind of closure, but there was nothing simplistic about the events unfolding around us. On 11 April 2002, almost two years after John's death, the Supreme Court upheld the decision of the High Court. The long-delayed Oireachtas inquiry could no longer continue its work. I was bitterly disappointed, but not surprised. There was nothing left to do except issue a statement thanking the sub-committee for its efforts to uncover the truth.

It's said that every cloud has a silver lining. On this occasion, it came into view when it was announced by Justice Minister John O'Donoghue that due to the failure of the Oireachtas probe, he was prepared to recommend a public tribunal into John's shooting. Taoiseach Bertie Ahern welcomed the decision, saying that he had always supported the Minister's wish to have a full investigation into what happened at Abbeylara.

When the phone rang and my solicitor informed me that we were going to have a full independent inquiry, I breathed a huge sigh of relief. Our persistence had paid off. The phone began to ring. Newspaper and television reporters had also heard the news and wanted to know how we felt. Exhaustion mostly, I wanted to say. I'd run a marathon and the finishing line was in sight.

'These questions need to be answered,' I told the reporters. 'We're waiting two years for answers. There's something wrong with the system if questions like these can't be answered.'

Justice Minister John O'Donoghue said that he was setting up the tribunal in the interests of truth, my family and the Garda Síochána.

All the evidence given to the tribunal would be published in a report when the inquiry was completed. The gardaí were also pleased with this decision. Garda Representative Association General Secretary P.J. Stone welcomed the Minister's call for an inquiry and said the gardaí were quite happy to answers any questions put by a tribunal.

Finally, there was hope that the truth could be revealed. We could only pray that it would bring some form of closure and acceptance of John's death.

Chapter Fourteen

During the course of its preliminary investigations the tribunal was furnished with over 200 witness statements, the vast majority of which were taken by members of the Garda Síochána during the course of an investigation carried out by Chief Superintendent (now Assistant Commissioner) Adrian Culligan. Potentially relevant witnesses were furnished with copies of their statements and requested to consider them and to clarify or add any matter deemed to be of relevance. In addition the tribunal was furnished with documentation submitted to the Oireachtas sub-committee established to investigate the Abbeylara incident. This documentation was supplied to the tribunal following the passing of appropriate resolutions of both Houses of the Oireachtas. The tribunal was also furnished with further information by the Garda Síochána, interested parties, members of the public and by experts retained by the tribunal during the course of the investigation.

– Barr Tribunal report, Memorandum on Procedures

So there we were again, my family, the gardaí, the legal teams, the media and the curious, all of us drawn together to replay those last twenty-five hours of my brother's life. I wondered if John was watching us from some distant sphere, as bemused as I was at how dramatically our ordinary lives had been transformed. The only newcomer to the scene was the chairman, Justice Robert Barr. He would be our final arbitrator. We had to place our trust in him and hope that he could seek out the truth from the mass of evidence he had to consider.

He travelled to Longford for the formal opening of the tribunal on 12 February 2003. In the same courtroom where John's inquest was held almost eighteen months previously, he received applications for legal representation from my family and the gardaí. We listened as he outlined the scope of his investigation. This was not a trial of alleged wrongdoing, he explained, but an examination of why the tragedy occurred and what we could learn from it. He sounded like a thoughtful and considerate judge, not intimidating, as I'd feared, but someone who would look carefully at all sides of the situation and bring in a balanced verdict.

When the tribunal began the investigative stage, it was located in Bow Street, close to the north side of the Liffey. This area is part of old Dublin and, although much of it has been modernised and refurbished, it still has all the hallmarks of a bygone era, with its cobbled streets and narrow side lanes. It was known for its whiskey distilling traditions, and the building chosen to house the tribunal was once used by Jameson Whiskey. Bow Street is also close to the Four Courts and was conveniently situated for the legal representatives. The old building was given a high-tech makeover to facilitate the inquiry. The format was similar to other tribunals I'd seen on television, the seating and tables laid out in theatre style, facing Justice Barr's bench. Each table had a desktop PC monitor. These were networked together and fed back to one big main screen to the right-hand side of the judge's bench. The stenographer sat in front of Justice Barr and faced everyone as she recorded the evidence each day. I'd expected wigs and gowns, but the barristers were dressed in suits, as were the members of the ERU. The only uniforms in evidence were worn by the gardaí, who dressed according to their rank. As always, they exuded power and authority. A seating area had been provided for journalists. I often saw guards sitting in an additional room fitted with a large television screen and speakers. The public seating area was also used by the some of the guards and ERU officers.

Dr Cullen was the first witness called. As John's GP since 1988, he was able to state categorically that he'd never found my brother to be aggressive, nor did he ever think he was likely to harm himself or anybody else. From the start of the stand-off, he'd been aware that the arrival of the gardaí could create difficulties and that John might be aggressive towards them in view of the incident with the mascot.

The facts surrounding the confiscation of John's shotgun in 1998 were closely examined. The by-now-retired guard Oliver Cassidy, who'd confiscated the gun, admitted to the tribunal that when he interviewed people in the village, they acknowledged that the stories they had heard were all second- or third-hand. In a small community, John was different. His illness set him apart, making everything he said or did open to scrutiny, judged by a different yardstick. Yet members of the Abbeylara gun club, Patrick Reilly and Bernard Brady, who used to go shooting with John, described him as always being careful with his gun, using it confidently and safely. According to Bernard, even when they were rough-shooting together he never felt in danger.

Dr Cullen described how John had approached him for a letter of support for the return of his gun and how he had postponed making a decision in the matter because of John's obvious distress over how he had been treated. He also spoke about John's visit to his surgery in 1998 on the morning after he'd been questioned in garda custody about the burning of the mascot. At that time, John had complained about general soreness around his neck and, in particular, along the left side of his upper neck. Dr Cullen had diagnosed a tenderness in that area which, in his opinion, would be consistent with some trauma or application of force. As John's animosity towards the guards was being linked to this incident, I had, at the start of the tribunal, called on those responsible for the act of vandalism to come forward and give direct evidence, thus clearing my brother's name. John had told me their names in confidence, and I remained true to my promise not to reveal their identity. They knew how much it would have meant to my family if they made this admission, but they paid no attention to my request.

From the beginning, any illusions that the tribunal would simply involve the reading of statements was quickly dispelled. It was to last 208 days and involved many tortuous hours of evidence. I'd fought hard to have this tribunal and, now that it was in place, I had to take the rough with the smooth. And there were rough days, when all I wanted to do was run from the building and bury my head under a pillow. Going over the minute details of John's medical records was harrowing: his voluntary admissions to St Loman's Hospital in Mullingar, his reaction to different drugs. Our father's death was seen as a prime trigger to his depression, causing him to be more emotionally vulnerable around the time of the anniversary.

Photographs were submitted to Justice Barr showing the state of our house when John finally left it. There were overturned tables and chairs, the television had been thrown on the ground, there were spent cartridges on the floor and damage caused to the internal walls of the house and a door by shotgun pellets. Worst of all were the photographs showing an armchair and the couch with the rug where he'd slept for those few hours during the siege.

Being exposed to the people who had cordoned off the house and conducted the stand-off was extremely disturbing. Occasionally I'd find myself sitting close to Michael Jackson and Aidan McCabe, the two ERU men who fired at John. It was deeply unsettling and upsetting to be so close to them. The constant tension during the three years since John's death had affected my health. I kept getting flashbacks. No matter what I was doing or how busy I was, the memory would suddenly hit me, and I'd see the guards surrounding the house, hear the loudhailer, the bullets, people scattering. This was the end result. All of us who had been involved in John's final illness, drawn together in this tension-filled arena to plead our case. Four bullets! I couldn't bear to look at their hands, yet I often wanted to speak to them, to ask if he had suffered much pain before he died. Had he uttered any last words, called out our names? But I couldn't bring myself to approach them, knowing I'd break down in tears if I attempted to speak to them.

Emotionally, I was being pulled in so many directions. During my time in Galway after John's death, my doctor recommended a psychiatrist, who diagnosed that I was suffering from post-traumatic stress. He recommended anti-depressants to help me cope. I went home and binned the tablets. What was the sense in suppressing what had happened? I needed to face into it. I'd seen what depression had done to John and had no intention of following a prescribed-drugs route. When I returned for my next consultation, I told the psychiatrist I'd taken evening primrose oil and multi-vitamins. He laughed and said I had a magic mind. But there was no magic, just the conviction that my family deserved answers. One day, another ERU man came up to me at the tribunal and apologised for what had happened. I asked him why he didn't tell the truth, thinking of the Culligan Report and the effect it had had on so many people who were close to John. I became quite upset and was unable to finish our conversation. I appreciated that the gardaí had also been affected by the tragedy. They had seen my brother's body sprawled before them. It was courageous for that officer to speak to me, and I appreciated the effort it took him. But he couldn't give me the answers I needed. He, like me, was locked into his personal position, supportive of his own colleagues and the decisions they took. There could be no middle ground between us.

Day after day of tribunal evidence followed. The publicity was constant. In the past, I'd often watched the media coverage of tribunals or court cases on television: the arrival of the key players, the legal teams and witnesses, the bereaved, the bewildered, the guilty. I'd viewed this unfolding scenario from the comfort of an armchair, never thinking for an instant that I or my extended family would be the ones filmed as we walked through the flashing cameras. Most days the television camera crews and photographers were waiting for my arrival. Some of them would actually run after me to get photographs. This was nerve-wracking. One day, I talked to a friendly photographer outside the tribunal offices. He advised me that the best approach was to stop and let them take the photographs. From then on, I did as he suggested, and this made things a little easier.

In the midst of all the formality of the tribunal surroundings, there was always a human touch, like Danny, the security man who let everyone into the building when we rang the buzzer. He was a kind and pleasant man who always had sweets for us on his desk and would take time to chat and make us feel welcome. Mary Simpson, an American woman I'd never met before the tribunal, sat beside me on a number of occasions. Like so many people, her family life had been touched by depression and, for this reason, she travelled twice from the USA to attend the proceedings. Some people came out of curiosity, others for support. They'd pass a kindly comment or squeeze my hand, but none of them encroached on my privacy or attempted to distract me from the cross-examinations.

My close friends had kept me going in the months following John's death. Just having them nearby forced me to my feet every morning. But another person was to return to my life, and he became my rock of support during the difficult days of the tribunal.

About a year after I first met Patrick and lost touch with him, I returned home for a weekend. A friend invited me to a party in Granard. To my surprise, Patrick was among the guests. We chatted briefly and casually. He was as friendly as ever and still seemed oblivious to my identity. The following day, I bumped into him when I was waiting for the bus back to Galway, and we arranged to see each other again. For a few weeks afterwards, I seemed to live in an oasis of my own making. I never mentioned the tragedy that had befallen my family to him, and he never brought up the subject. He must have been the only person in Ireland who hadn't heard about Abbeylara and all that followed. We'd meet like any other young couple and talk about the events of the day, films, books, the kind of music we enjoyed. I was reluctant to break my silence, but I knew this brief carefree relationship couldn't last much longer. He could pick up a newspaper any morning and see my photograph, hear something on the radio or television. He was still travelling abroad on business and didn't have daily contact with our mutual acquaintances, but if he did meet them and mentioned that he was seeing me, he would certainly hear about John. Then all he had to do was search the internet, where the Culligan Report, with all its cruel detail, was available.

Finally, one night, I told him everything. He was stunned by my revelation, unable at first to take it in. I showed him photographs of John, introduced him to Rose. I wondered if he would end our relationship in case he was drawn into the stressful journey I had embarked upon. He showed no signs of doing so and was fully supportive of my desire to establish an independent inquiry.

Patrick always accompanied me to the tribunal hearings when he was able to take time off work. He preferred to stay in the background, and I was very protective of his privacy. I ensured that he was never photographed or filmed accompanying me into the proceedings but, once inside, he was there to hold my arm or offer his shoulder when I needed it. Meeting Patrick restored some form of normality to my life. I was capable of feeling emotions other than anger, grief and loss. Somewhere, at the end of the dark tunnel where my future lay, I could see a glimmer of light.

My only regret at persisting at getting the public hearing was the pain it caused my mother, my extended family and John's friends. This feeling was reinforced when I watched Rose sobbing as she was cross-examined in the witness box. She was treated courteously by Mr McGrath, Senior Counsel for the Tribunal, but going over the last moments she spent with John has always been extremely emotional for her. The ordeal of repeating it in the pressurised environment of the tribunal was almost more than she could endure. The following extract recalls how she parted from her son, not realising that she would never speak to him again.

Q. If I could just go back slightly, just one other point. When you were leaving the house, did John say anything to you as you were leaving the house?

A. He said good luck or good-bye, something like that, yeah.

Q. He said good-bye?

A. Yeah.

Q. Can you remember when John went outside the door to discharge the shots, did he bring the belt with him or did he leave it on the table, can you remember that?

A. I don't know, he probably left it on the table.

Q. What about the box of cartridges, did he bring those outside the door with him when he discharged the shots?

A. One or two he brought out, yes, he had the box inside, yes.

Q. Can I take it that when he took the gun out of the locker and brought it into the kitchen, can you remember was the gun loaded or unloaded when he brought the gun into the kitchen?

A. I don't remember.

Q. You don't remember, I see. You think he may have taken

one or two cartridges with him outside?
A. Yeah.
Q. Did he leave the box of cartridges on the table, can you remember?
A. He did, yeah.
Q. When he discharged the shots and came back into the kitchen, can you recollect did he reload the gun at that stage?
A. No, he didn't, it was opened.
Q. The gun was open, is that right?
A. Yeah.
Q. That is in the broken open position?
A. Yes.
Q. When he asked you to go up to your sister's for a while, when that conversation was taking place, can you recollect whether the gun was loaded or unloaded at that stage?
A. I would say it was open all the time.
Q. It was open all the time, so when you were leaving the house, was the gun open?
A. It was, yes, I seen it on the chair beside—
Q. Do you know, could you see the barrels of the gun?
A. I could. I could see it open, yes.
Q. Were there any cartridges in the barrels of the gun?
A. No, it was empty.
Q. It was empty?
A. Yeah.
Q. Can we take it that when you were leaving the house, he said good-bye to you, the gun was broken open and it was not loaded, is that your evidence?
A. Yeah.
Q. I see. Would you like to take a break for a few moments, Mrs Carthy? Would you like a break?

Despite the emotional impact this examination had on Rose, she was anxious to clear up the perception that she had been ordered from the house by her son at gunpoint. Somehow, she held herself together, and the cross-examination continued. The following short extract refers to the arrival of the garda to my aunt's house and was again conducted by Mr McGrath.

> Q. As I understand it, Mrs Carthy, you have no clear recollection of anything further that may have been said to the gardaí, is my understanding correct, apart from John having the gun in the house and discussing the medication he was on. Can you remember anything else?
>
> A. No, I can't remember anything else.
>
> Q. Can you remember anything about questions that you may have been asked by the gardaí who arrived?
>
> A. They said he would be all right, that he would be okay, nothing would happen to him.
>
> The Chairman: They said?
>
> A. They said, yeah.
>
> Q. The Chairman: That he would be okay, he would be all right?
>
> A. Yes.
>
> Q. Mr McGrath: They were reassuring you, is that right, Mrs Carthy?
>
> A. Yes.
>
> Q. I see.
>
> A. That is why I called them the first time.
>
> Q. I understand.
>
> A. I wanted help from them, I didn't want him killed.

I've always believed that the visibility of the initial squad cars that arrived on the scene and the obvious presence of guards had created confrontation rather than mediation. But Superintendent Shelly was of the opposite opinion. I listened carefully as he outlined his defence. At the start of the stand-off, he had believed the situation to be so dangerous that he'd contacted a number of stations looking for armed back-up even before he arrived in Abbeylara. Yet Superintendent Shelly didn't know anything about John. He had no details of his medical problems and, of course, knew nothing at the time about his alleged mistreatment by the gardaí. All he knew was that an armed confrontation was taking place. He reported his concerns to Chief Superintendent Patrick Tansey and was in complete agreement with the discussions that followed between the Chief Superintendent and Assistant Commissioner Hickey. This conversation resulted in a decision being made to call in the ERU. Superintendent Shelly never had second thoughts about this decision. As he explained, the decision evolved from his own assessment of the danger John posed.

'They made it on the information – on the basis of the information I gave them and I was happy with that,' he told the tribunal, adding that if the situation had gone on much further, 'maybe I would have suggested it to either Chief Superintendent Tansey or Assistant Commissioner Hickey that consideration be given to it.'

Before the ERU arrived, Superintendent Shelly made efforts to negotiate with John by addressing him through a loudhailer and ordering him to throw down his gun. As far as I'm concerned, by the time the chief negotiator, Michael Jackson, arrived, the damage was done. What should have been a low-key approach had been turned into a highly charged confrontation which continued to escalate out of control.

One very contentious issue examined was why John hadn't received the cigarettes he requested. Justice Barr, an ex-smoker himself, understood the dependency of a heavy smoker and the effects of nicotine withdrawal. Yet, the gardaí insisted it was too risky to find some way of handing them over. However, when it came to cutting off our television signal, this was easily done when John was sleeping. Superintendent Byrne was worried that John might hear something on television that could inflame the situation. Had he ever heard of nicotine-withdrawal symptoms – headaches, anxiety, nausea and the craving for more tobacco? Why could they not have been left on the doorstep or some other convenient location when John was sleeping? Superintendent Byrne, however, was of the opinion that John couldn't have had a craving for cigarettes at that stage because he was sleeping. I thought this was an incredible comment and was hardly the point. John was bound to wake up, and cigarettes would be the first thing he'd want.

Justice Barr stated that if the guards had wanted to give cigarettes to John, it would have been possible. He refused to accept reasons or excuses. The tribunal was becoming highly emotional, especially when I listened to Superintendent Byrne give evidence that the guard who dropped us off at Devines' house went on his break. The senior guards at the scene were never told where he went, and this resulted in a delay of over an hour and a half before Pepper was contacted. So many mistakes were made that night, simple mistakes, yet what a difference it could have made if they'd never been allowed to happen.

Superintendent Byrne also felt that he didn't have to justify the reasons why I wasn't allowed speak to John. By then, I should have been used to the accusation that I was drunk at the scene, yet when I heard it repeated at the tribunal, the humiliation and sense of helplessness was as severe as the first time I'd read it in the Culligan Report. It was now being repeated to an assembled gathering of the public, the media and the people closest to me, but there was nothing I could do except sit there and listen as Superintendent Byrne described how he believed I was under the influence of alcohol. I was swaying, he claimed, and my speech was 'quite slurred'. However, answering Justice Barr, he stated that he did not smell alcohol and that I didn't have to be supported by Patricia Leavey. He accepted that he did not indicate my 'insobriety' to any member of my family, 'even in the most discreet way'. Nor did he suggest that I could go off and have a cup of coffee, insisting that he had no wish to upset us any more than we were already.

But it was clear from his evidence that in the small hours of Holy Thursday morning, when myself, Pepper and Patricia left Devines' house and returned to the scene, a decision had already been made between himself and the negotiator, Sergeant Jackson, that I wouldn't be allowed to speak to John. The reason given was that John had asked to communicate only with Pepper and they didn't want to spring any surprises on him. At that time, I'd no idea if John even knew I was in Abbeylara. When the guards refused to allow me to go down with Pepper, I naturally became distressed, but Superintendent Byrne contended that this display of emotion was down to alcohol.

He admitted to the tribunal that when he was making his statement to the Culligan Inquiry team, he described me as being distressed. When asked by one of the team to elaborate on what he meant by 'distressed' he replied, 'She was drunk.' According to him, the interviewer then told him, 'That is what you had better put down.'

After failing to reach John, I had been persuaded to sit in a garda jeep with Patricia while Pepper tried talking to John. Detective Garda Campbell, who was also in the jeep, backed up Superintendent Byrne's claim. At first, when he was asked if I was 'anything other than agitated and upset', he answered, 'No.' When he was questioned further, he stated that he smelled alcohol from me and that I was fidgety. This convinced him that I was 'under the influence of alcohol'. He also formed the impression that I was annoyed about not being allowed speak to John and then claimed he was '100% sure' that I was under the influence of drink.

The urge to stand up and accuse them of lying raged inside me but, no matter what they said or how they elaborated this falsehood, I kept my head down and didn't respond. I wasn't prepared to let myself or my family down, nor did I want to supply tomorrow's media headlines.

There was no escaping the publicity surrounding the tribunal. Some days, I was too embarrassed to go out in public after reading the newspapers or hearing the news, especially when the reports were broadcast every hour. This was so far removed from what had once been my normal life. In fact, it was becoming increasingly difficult to remember I'd ever had a life that wasn't consumed by John's death and its consequences.

The drink accusation failed to go away. This was brought home to me yet again one weekend when I met some friends in one of the local pubs in Abbeylara. On leaving the pub, a garda car drew up in front of my car. I could see two guards inside. I found it difficult to look at a uniformed guard without memories of the stand-off welling up inside me, and there was something startling about the speed with which the car had approached us. One of the guards walked towards the passenger door of my car and shouted in at me that I was not to start the engine. I couldn't believe what I was hearing. When I asked why, he replied, still shouting, 'Because you have been drinking.'

As the designated driver, I had been on mineral water for the evening. I assured the guard that I had not been drinking, but he repeated the accusation and again ordered me not to start the engine. My friends were horrified listening to this exchange, which was obviously meant to embarrass me. He then went on to say that he actually saw me drinking. I knew this was pure rubbish, but he paid no attention to my protests. Finally, unable to tolerate being so humiliated, I urged him to give me a breathalyser test. When he refused to do so, I started up the engine. I then repeated my request for a breathalyser. He refused to answer me or order me to blow into the bag. The other guard made no attempt to speak either. I told them to leave me alone and drove off. Outwardly, I tried to remain calm, but I felt very shaky inside, not knowing how the episode would conclude.

The guards watched as I drove away, then began to drive behind me. I dropped my friends off at their house and continued on home, conscious all the time of the squad-car lights in my rear-view mirror. I knew if I made the slightest mistake I would immediately be pulled over. Any pleasure I'd felt during my evening out was gone. The guards parked outside my home for a few minutes before driving off. It was a petty act, yet it brought home the horrible truth that I was under observation. Abbeylara was becoming too small to contain the hostility the guards felt towards me.

Patrick had come into my life at a very difficult time. I'd fallen in love with him and was beginning to understand that in the midst of grief and turmoil, happiness can also shine through. I made a decision to move to Meath. I chose Meath because it was close to Abbeylara and it would be easy to visit Rose regularly. My heart would always belong to my village, but there were too many painful memories everywhere I turned. This latest action by the gardaí reopened all the old wounds. The time had come to begin the next stage of my life.

Chapter Fifteen

Mr Frederick Lanceley, formerly of the FBI, stated in evidence that he coined the term 'suicide by cop', in response to a situation he witnessed where he believed that individuals who were clearly suicidal were demanding that the police kill them and were manipulating situations to the point where the police had no choice but to use deadly force. He explained to the tribunal 'the instrumentality of their deaths was not drugs, a gun, a rope or jumping from a bridge but the police. The incident was not a suicide by gun or suicide by jumping it was a suicide by cop.' In his view, suicide by cop refers to a suicide where the person wants to die but prefers to have the police kill him or her as opposed to killing himself or herself.
– Barr Tribunal report, Chapter 14

The gardaí hoped to prove that John wanted them to kill him. The 'suicide by cop' theory was aired regularly during the hearing. A number of expert witnesses came to the tribunal to give their opinions. Former FBI member Frederick Lanceley, who had coined the term 'suicide by cop', was a witness for the gardaí. Author of a book called *On-Scene Guide for Crisis Negotiators*, he declared at the outset of his cross-examination that he felt the Irish people didn't care about the safety of their police officers. Presumably, this was due to the public demand for an independent inquiry. He criticised the positioning of the negotiation post, believing it to be a constant reminder to John that he was under siege. He also believed Detective Inspector Jackson didn't have enough assistance and that three or four more negotiators had been needed.

His opinion was that John had a fixed and premeditated plan to end his own life by garda fire. I listened in disbelief to this well-groomed man who sat with a rigid posture while giving evidence. In his opinion, John's suicide plan was disrupted over the course of the stand-off, and he was forced to improvise by leaving the house. If this had occurred in the USA rather than Abbeylara, and John had come to the window pointing a shotgun at the negotiator, he would have been lawfully shot on the spot by a sniper, he said. If this was how US cops dealt with victims of depression, I wondered why it would be necessary for three or four extra negotiators to be on hand.

Other experts gave their views on the suicide-by-cop theory. Dr Douglas Turkington, a UK consultant psychiatrist and senior lecturer in liaison psychiatry, believed that John's suicidal intent was personality-driven and that he orchestrated the situation which resulted in the police being forced to shoot him. However, he conceded that John's mental state could have made him indifferent to the outcome of his actions. Dr Ian MacKenzie, a chartered forensic and occupational psychologist, was of the opinion that John intended ending his life, but believed his suicide plan was only formulated on the afternoon of his death.

This was rejected by Dr John Sheehan, a consultant psychiatrist, who stated, 'I do not think that Mr Carthy's behaviour on leaving the house is consistent with a suicide attempt. It appears that he walked past three or more armed ERU men. Had he wanted to commit suicide, it is likely that he could have precipitated a confrontation immediately on leaving the house . . . His behaviour is consistent with an elated mood, demonstrating impaired judgment and false self-confidence.'

It was difficult to sit there and listen to experts presenting contradictory but well-formulated views. I was terrified that 'suicide by cop' would be John's epitaph and that Judge Barr would come to this conclusion. Thankfully, he ultimately dismissed it as pure speculation and believed it was impossible to know what was going on in John's mind at the time.

When Mr Lanceley was asked by our senior counsel, Mr Gageby, if he would use the Abbeylara siege as an instructive case in his future seminars, he replied, 'Yes, sir. I don't see anything here that is terribly inconsistent with suicide-by-cop.' Mr Gageby then asked him, 'Will you say anything to your students about the issue of why the Carthy family weren't told about Mr Carthy's looking for a solicitor?'

A. Sorry, sir?
Q. Are you aware that the Carthy family were never told that Mr Carthy, the deceased, was looking for a solicitor?
A. That he?
Q. Was looking for a solicitor. Are you aware of that?
A. No, sir.

Not providing a solicitor was a recurring and sensitive issue for the gardaí. Although they had been exonerated in the Culligan Report, it had contained that one criticism. During Superintendent Byrne's evidence, I was shocked to discover that he did consider obtaining a solicitor from the locality but had ruled this out on account of the way John was treating his friends and family who had attempted to speak with him. Again, this emphasised the lack of understanding of the volatile behaviour of a mentally ill person. The people John rejected when they tried to speak to him at the negotiating position – Pepper, Sean Farrell and his cousin Thomas – were close to John. He had the utmost respect for them. The fact that he refused to engage with them or reacted in a hostile manner was indicative of his illness rather than his personality. It should never have been used as a reason not to seek the advice of a solicitor. Frederick Lanceley conceded that it would have helped negotiations if a solicitor had been provided and that this should have been the scene commander's decision. As far as he was concerned, there wouldn't have been a problem with various friends and relations, including myself, being brought down to the scene.

I attended the hearings at every available opportunity, and if I missed a day, I read the transcripts, which were e-mailed to me daily. Reading through these pages and pages of detailed information was often quite challenging but, despite this and the difficulties of listening to witness evidence and media reports, I was determined to keep abreast with everything that was going on. I had to remain on top of things, partly so that, if necessary, I could immediately go to Dublin to see my legal team. I also needed to be available to the media.

Being in attendance undoubtedly made it easier to follow the proceedings. I could address any questions directly to my legal team, who guided me through this maze of information. But I took no pleasure in the proceedings, no satisfaction as points were scored or lost in cross-examination. John had shared my life for twenty-six years, but since his death he seemed to belong to everyone. He had become a cause for those who believed that the gardaí had mishandled the situation. In the view of those who favoured the opinion of the guards, he was seen as an out-of-control manic depressive who had endangered their lives. He was a source of debate for those with differing opinions, a complex case history to be argued over and analysed for the medical experts involved. All the time, I tried to hold on to the person I'd known and loved. Sometimes it seemed that the unexpected tide surrounding his death would sweep even my cherished memories away with it. I desperately tried to cling on to the good times, when life had been so much simpler.

Chapter Sixteen

In summary, I recognise that I may have been unfair in concluding that the conduct of Mr Rogers appeared to have amounted to attempted bullying tactics for whatever motive and that his behaviour is out of kilter with other counsel appearing at this tribunal. If I was wrong in harbouring and expressing such thoughts, then I regret having done so. As already stated, I hope that for the remainder of the tribunal there will be a better understanding between Mr Rogers and I. Both of us should exercise vigilance in that regard and for my part I shall do so.

– Barr Tribunal report, Appendix 7

Any adjournments to the tribunal made me nervous. On a few occasions, I was afraid the proceedings would be brought to a premature end, especially when heated exchanges took place between the legal teams for the gardaí and Justice Barr. In particular, John Rogers strongly objected to Justice Barr's practice of interrupting cross-examinations when the chairman wanted to clarify points in his own mind. He believed such questions should only be asked at the end of each cross-examination, but the chairman refused to do so, claiming that that would only involve delays and evidence having to be repeated. I witnessed two strong-willed men squaring up to each other and, remembering the successful efforts by the gardaí to end the Oireachtas investigation, was afraid that this could happen again before any conclusions were reached.

In mid-July, a heated argument broke out between Diarmuid McGuinness, counsel for the Garda Commissioner, and the chairman. Mr McGuinness claimed that Justice Barr had already made up his mind on crucial aspects of the inquiry. This occurred during the cross-examination of one of the ERU members, Detective Garda Gerry Russell, who had been the ERU tactical team leader. Justice Barr asked why both he and the negotiator, Michael Jackson, decided to locate the negotiation post only yards from the house. Expert evidence to be brought before the inquiry would prove that eye-to-eye confrontation with John was the last route that should have been taken. John Rogers, senior counsel for the guards, immediately intervened and declared that no expert evidence had been circulated regarding the wisdom of this tactic and accused the judge of forming conclusions before this evidence had even been given. Justice Barr denied that he had formed any conclusions. His function was to get to the facts. John Rogers demanded that the evidence be circulated, and the tribunal was adjourned until 11:00 a.m. the following morning. I'd no idea if it would reconvene and spent a sleepless night worrying about what the next day would bring.

But the tribunal continued to move on, a slow, tortuous process that left no stone unturned in assessing the truth. John Rogers was tough and aggressive in his cross-questioning, sometimes to the point where Justice Barr had to intervene and demand that he stop bullying witnesses. In turn, Mr Rogers made the same accusation to the judge and said he was being treated with 'contempt and disdain.' Being subjected to his cross-examination proved to be one of my most distressing experiences at the tribunal. Some days were more traumatic than others. I went into shock when the state pathologist, John Harbison, on being questioned about the bullet wounds sustained by John, pointed out the entry and exit angles of the bullets. The jeans John wore on the day he died were held up for examination. I'd heard evidence that the denim 'fluttered' when the first bullet struck his leg and was sickened by the picture this created in my mind. When Professor Harbison explained the numbering system he used to identify the wounds on the front and back of John's body, I had to fight off an attack of nausea as I listened to the cold hard facts about which bones, muscles and vital organs were struck by bullets. Patrick, who was with me on that day, put his arms around me and comforted me. This helped me to gather myself together and refocus on the pathologist's analysis.

Initially, there was some confusion about the number of bullets fired. Professor Milroy, another expert witness and a professor of forensic pathology, had expressed an opinion in an earlier report to the tribunal that one of the wounds might represent a fifth bullet. He described the appearance of 'more holes than bullets fired' as a 'not uncommon problem' presented to pathologists from time to time. Justice Barr was particularly keen to explore the possibility that a fifth bullet could have been fired. Among the armed non-ERU guards at the scene when John left the house was Detective Sergeant Foley. In the aftermath of the shooting, he had expressed criticism of the ERU officers for allowing John to walk as far as he did through the inner police cordon. As John paid no attention to the ERU men positioned by the gate and continued walking, having ignored their commands to lay down his gun, Sergeant Foley said to Garda Boland, who was standing close to him, 'We are going to have to do it,' meaning that he would have to shoot. Both guards stated in evidence that they feared for their lives. Sergeant Foley was about to fire when John was shot from behind. Afterwards, the ERU weapons were examined by a ballistics expert who verified the fact that four shots were fired, but none of the guns carried by the local gardaí were checked. Nor was a check made on ammunition issued or returned to the station, despite garda regulations stating that this should be done at the end of an armed operation. Therefore, no records were furnished to the tribunal regarding ammunition which had been in the possession of the non-ERU armed guards. It seemed a reasonable desire on the part of the judge to, as he put it, 'postulate for the moment that there might have been a fifth shot'.

Professor Harbison had also wondered whether or not a fifth bullet had been fired, but both he and Professor Milroy eventually concluded that only four bullets had been used. The wound in John's calf was more likely to be a re-entry from the third wound he suffered because, as Professor Harbison stated, 'that keeps it within the four bullets'. When Justice Barr responded, 'Don't worry about the number of bullets. Is it possible that there could have been a fifth bullet fired by a non-ERU officer?' John Rogers angrily intervened and stated that Justice Barr was making entirely outrageous comments. He was ordered to sit down, but he eventually stormed out of the tribunal, a dramatic exit that achieved the desired headlines. It was a shocking and eye-opening experience to watch his behaviour and listen to his comments, which Justice Barr described as 'gratuitously insensitive'. The gardaí still had one other senior counsel and a barrister in attendance, so his exit didn't hold up proceedings. However, this was just before Christmas, and the tribunal was then adjourned until the new year.

On our return, the situation became even more tense. Again, I feared that the entire proceedings would end prematurely, but Justice Barr remained adamant that he would conduct the tribunal in his own way, which meant intervening in cross-examination when he wanted to clarify a point or pursue a certain line of enquiry. He didn't accept Mr Rogers' contention that all questioning should be left entirely to counsel for the tribunal. Despite continuing protests from the garda legal team over the issue of the 'fifth bullet', the judge ruled that he would continue carrying on with this inquiry.

After he made this ruling, the remaining members of the legal teams for the gardaí withdrew from the tribunal. The atmosphere, which had been heated and angry on many occasions, was now openly hostile as the legal teams and over twenty gardaí involved failed to turn up on the following day. We'd come so far – over ten months of cross-examinations, arguments, analysis, conflicting theories. Was it all to end in this disgraceful fashion, stopped in its tracks once again by the actions of the gardaí? I made a statement to the press to that effect but, to my relief, the row was soon over. Justice Barr declared that 'the possibility of Mr Carthy having been wounded by a fifth bullet is no longer an issue in the tribunal'.

It was back to business as usual.

On 8 March 2004, the *Irish Independent* ran a feature on the breakdown costs of the tribunal, which had been provided under the Freedom of Information Act. I was staggered by the costs of legal and consultancy fees. One consultant employed to work on the inquiry had been paid more than €163,000 for his work. Expert witnesses Alan Bailey and Frederick Lanceley received over €207,000 between them. IT consultants PricewaterhouseCoopers received €189,579, and the payments to the eight firms employed by the tribunal, including a forensic psychologist, consultant engineer and consulting forensic scientists, totalled €477,020. In comparison, witness expenses amounted to €4,569.

Many times, I'd felt as if I was living in a fantasy world. Like Alice, I'd gone through the looking glass and was in a wonderland where everything was obscured. I thought back to the time before John's shooting when my mother was worried about financing the move to her new house. She approached the local bank to borrow a small sum of money for furniture and fittings and was refused the loan – such an insignificant sum when balanced against the vast amount of money being spent on seeking answers to her son's death.

Chapter Seventeen

Q. My name is John Rogers and I appear for the gardaí who were at the scene. In relation to the evening you came up from Galway, the Thursday evening, it seems a little surprising that you didn't go immediately to see your mother. Did you have a reason for that?

A. No, I was more concerned about John, and I knew my mother was safe because she was with – she was okay, like, there was nothing to worry about because she was with other family members and I was more interested in getting to talk to John.

Q. I know, but wasn't your mother and the other family members, weren't they in the best position to tell you what John's predicament was?

A. But I had no reason – I didn't want to go and see them, I just wanted to go and see John and the gardaí were there to tell me what was going on.

– Extract from my cross-examination on 26 June 2003

One of my abiding memories of the tribunal was my two days of giving evidence, which took place over 25–6 June 2003. In the days leading up to the cross-examination, I became increasingly nervous at the thought of what lay ahead. I was afraid I'd be unable to answer questions or that I'd break down in front of everyone, even faint under the strain. I hardly slept the night before I was due to appear. My mind raced back over the terrifying hours of the stand-off, remembering the evening I received the news and the sequence of events as they unfolded. I wondered if there was anything else I could have done to prevent the final devastating outcome. In my heart, I knew I'd always been there for John, but the guilt I felt over his death was insidious and could strike at the most unexpected times. I'd heard that this was a common reaction when people lost a loved family member in tragic circumstances, and I accepted that this guilt was a burden I'd have to carry until such time as I was able to deal rationally with my emotions. Lying there in the dawning light of a new day, I wondered if that release would ever come. Then I moved back in time and sought relief in childhood memories, happy days in Galway when it seemed as if John's illness had stabilised and his life was on an even keel. It was after five in the morning when I dozed off, only to awake shortly afterwards to face the journey to Dublin.

On the first day of giving evidence, the tribunal personnel helped me to feel at ease. Mr Michael McGrath, senior counsel for the tribunal, questioned me in detail about my life with John. The events leading to the stand-off were closely examined, in particular John's animosity towards the guards, as outlined in the following short extract from his cross-examination.

> *Q. Again, during this period in summer and autumn 1998, we have heard evidence of the goat mascot that was down in the village and which was burned by fire or destroyed by fire and we have also heard evidence of John's arrest in connection with that incident. I just want to ask you some questions generally. Prior to this incident, when John was arrested in September 1998, do you know did John have any contact with An Garda Síochána?*

A. No, he never had any real contact, maybe going into the barracks to get a form maybe for a driving licence or—

Q. Or his gun licence?

A. Gun licence, that would be about it.

Q. Again, prior to this event, did he have any opinions or did he express any opinions to you about the gardaí, about members of An Garda Síochána?

A. No, he never had any cause to mention them or anything.

Q. We know that he was arrested and was detained for some hours but he wasn't charged and he was subsequently released from custody some time after 10:00 on the night in question. Did you become aware of that?

A. Yeah, he rang me that night to tell me about the burning of the goat, he actually told me the morning that it was burned what happened. He told me who did it and he told me not to tell anyone their names and he was telling me about the mistreatment he received in the garda station.

Q. You said in your statement that John – it would seem that his attitude to the gardaí seemed to change somewhat, is that correct, after this?

A. Yeah, he didn't trust them and he kind of feared them as well after what happened to him in the garda station.

Q. He didn't make any formal complaint about what happened to him, did he?

A. He was kind of afraid to in a way, he didn't want to go against the gardaí. But he actually went to his local doctor, Dr Cullen, the following morning and he was sent for X-ray after that.

Q. Would it be fair to say that no either formal or informal complaint was made by either John or by any member of the family to the gardaí concerning his allegations of mistreatment in custody?

A. No, he never made a formal complaint.
Q. No member of the family took the matter up with the gardaí either, would that be fair to say?
A. No, he wouldn't allow us to, he didn't want us to.

My public request to the men involved in the mascot-burning incident had gone unanswered. It would have been such a small yet significant gesture to make. Instead, they maintained their silence and, although no charges were ever brought against my brother for this act of vandalism, his name was never cleared.

Mr McGrath also questioned me closely about the Christmas in Galway when John became ill.

Q. The date of discharge is 6 January 1999. Then we see the reasons for his admission, that he presented to the accident and emergency accompanied by his sister with complaints of poor sleep for the previous two weeks, feelings of irritability and exhaustion. He also described poor concentration. I would like to deal with the complaints that were recorded there. He was complaining of poor sleep to the people on the accident and emergency department, was that something that you were aware of?
A. Yeah, he wasn't sleeping very well.
Q. Then it refers to feelings of irritability and exhaustion. Was the irritability – was that obvious or could you see that he was irritable in some way?
A. He was slightly irritable and he was really tired as well because he wasn't sleeping.
Q. I see. He also described poor concentration. Then the note records the previous history of his illness and medication. If I could just go down to the findings on admission. That he was 'neatly dressed, well groomed man.

Maintained eye contact. Speech was rapid and he was easily distractible. He was not suicidal. He described his mood as grand. Objectively he was mildly elated. Concentration was poor and no formal thought disorder was elicited.' Was that something that was discussed with you by the doctors, can you remember, what they found?

A. Yeah, they would have told me that.

Q. It goes on to deal with the condition on discharge and then it says, in the second sentence there: *'denied suicide ideation, death wish, or thoughts of self-harm, seemed motivated to abstain from alcohol.'* Just to deal with the last sentence. Was alcohol a factor at that time in December 1998, was it a factor, in your view, did it play a role in relation to his mood and his condition?

A. No, he just would have been like any normal young lad going for a few pints and that. But it wouldn't be good to drink too much alcohol, taking tablets.

Q. I see. So, this particular admission in December 1998, alcohol was not a big issue as far as you were concerned?

A. No.

Q. And then we see *'prognosis and recommendations'* and I would like to ask you about this. It says: *'prognosis is guarded due to dubious compliance with medications. To attend day hospital daily for monitoring of his progress.'* You have given evidence that as far as you were concerned he was quite compliant with the medication which he had been prescribed. Was this discussed with you, the fact that somebody had formed a view that there may have been dubious compliance with medication at that time?

A. No.

Q. That wasn't mentioned to you?

A. No.

Q. Were you happy from your observations that he was taking his medication?
A. Yeah, because I'd seen him taking it, that is how I knew.

Despite the 'dubious-compliance claim', John was always aware of the importance of taking his medication regularly. But being cross-examined so closely about this difficult period in his life was tough. In the beginning, before Rose and I had a better understanding of his illness, we had found it hard to know how to cope with such episodes. But John's knowledge of his depression and our own experience gained over the years had helped us through that particular time when he admitted himself to hospital in Galway. As I answered the barrister's questions, I remembered how my sympathy for John had been mixed with disappointment that the Christmas I'd planned so thoroughly was spoiled. It was a human reaction, yet how unimportant such considerations now seemed when all I wanted to do was to take that time back again, no matter how painful or demanding the circumstances.

John had received great comfort and support from the day hospital, and it was during those weeks when he attended it as an outpatient that he made the decision to move to Galway. He had been so optimistic then, planning a fresh start, looking forward to making new friends who would know nothing about his past medical history. There would be no stigma to mark him out as different, no cloud of shame and an unresolved accusation hanging over him.

During my two days of giving evidence, the incident in Galway city when John was taken into custody to be examined by a doctor was addressed by three separate senior counsels, Mr McGrath for the tribunal, Mr McGuinness for the Garda Commissioner and Mr Rogers for the gardaí. My memories of our time in Galway were becoming bittersweet, dominated by this one event. What had been a low-key incident between us had assumed a significance neither of could ever have foreseen, even in our worst nightmares. This extract is from my cross-examination by John Rogers and is based around evidence given by Garda O'Boyle, the female guard I'd spoken to in Galway when John became elated.

Q. So the result of this was that John was arrested and in effect, on your say so, that you were worried about him, isn't that right?

A. I was worried, yes.

Q. You see, this witness, in giving evidence before the Chairman, reported you as saying that you were concerned that John would harm himself. That he was suicidal, isn't that correct, because this is what this witness has said?

A. That is what that witness has said, but I don't recall saying he was suicidal.

Q. You see, can I ask you – did you ever form the view that John might have been suicidal at any time before his death?

A. Never.

Q. You never thought he was suicidal?

A. Never.

Q. Do you think Garda O'Boyle had any reason to make this up?

A. No.

Chairman: Might you have said something to that effect in an effort to encourage the guards to co-operate in having John seen by a doctor?

A. Yeah, I might have done, because you see in the beginning they weren't willing to help, they said there was nothing they could do and, of course, maybe I did say it, just to get them to help me. I don't know, like, I can't remember.

Q. You see, now you are telling the Chairman that maybe you did say it, just to get something to happen?

A. I never said in the beginning that I didn't say it, I said I can't remember saying it; maybe I did say it. I am not calling the woman a liar, if she said it, I may have said it.

Q. Yes. It is a very serious thing to say to a guard, 'my brother is suicidal, I want him arrested' and that is what you did that night, is it not?

A. I didn't say it like that, according to her evidence, I didn't go and say, 'my brother is suicidal, I want him arrested.' I asked for help.

Q. That is the effect of what you did and it was fully explained to you on the night by the garda concerned, that you expressing fears for his life and safety, you saying that he was suicidal, you saying that you might find him in the river, that she then explained to you that she could arrest him so that he could be examined by a doctor. That is what happened and you know that is what happened because it was explained to you fully at the time, and we have gone through it now and you agree all of what was said by Garda O'Boyle was said; isn't that correct?

A. But I don't recall saying the bit about him being suicidal. If I don't recall it, you can't make me recall.

Q. Sorry?

A. If I can't recall something, there is no way I can be made recall it because I just can't recall.

Q. Well, I am not trying to make you do anything but what I must ask you is questions that will elicit what actually happened.

A. But you keep asking me the same question 'did I say he was suicidal' and I just already told you I don't recall saying it.

Chairman: Mr Rogers, the witness has said that she is not suggesting that the garda is making this up or that anything she has said in evidence is untrue. She is saying she can't recall saying that. She has also agreed that she may have said something to that effect with a view to encouraging the gardaí to help her to get a doctor to see her brother. That is what she achieved in the end, but she didn't achieve it in the beginning because, if I accept her evidence, the gardaí were not too keen to become involved at the beginning, understandably enough. But they became involved as a result of what Ms Carthy told them.

A. There is an answer there as well, sorry.

Q. Ms Carthy, it is a very serious thing to have your brother arrested if he wasn't suicidal.

A. You can't expect any one person to recall everything. That garda has written there question 16, or line 16, 'I cannot recall anything further than that, no'. She didn't remember everything.

Q. It is a very serious thing to have your brother arrested; isn't that right?

A. Not if it is to help him.

Q. Of course. You knew that John had an aversion to the gardaí. According to yourself, he had an aversion to the gardaí; isn't that right?

A. He had a fear of them and he didn't fully trust them, but I was with him at all times and I knew he was going to be safe and he wasn't on his own at any time, only when he was with the doctor.

Q. You see, if we just look further on in this transcript—

Chairman: Mr Rogers, I don't want to curtail your examination of this witness, but I don't see that there is any issue involved here. There is no doubt of it that Mr Carthy was unwell at that time.

Mr Rogers: There is—

Chairman: *I have no doubt certainly on the evidence of this witness and others.*

Mr Rogers: *I am putting all of these questions to this witness for a purpose, Chairman, you can take it for certain that I have a purpose.*

Chairman: *Very well.*

Q. *When we look at this – the garda recalls at question 297 in her answer that 'John was annoyed at the fact that his sister had asked us for help', and she records then that he did go voluntarily; isn't that right?*

A. *That's right.*

Q. *She does also record that she arrested him. There is a question 306 where Garda O'Boyle was asked: 'Q. Was there any reaction during that period of time to his sister, did he have any conversation with his sister during that period of time before you went to the patrol car? A. I do remember him saying to her that he wouldn't forgive her for what she had done. I don't remember exactly where he said that to her, but I do know that he was annoyed at having been arrested.' Do you recall John being annoyed to the point where he said that to you?*

A. *I don't recall him saying that, but I know he was annoyed and naturally enough he wasn't himself, he was depressed and he just was annoyed with me for contacting the gardaí, but he thanked me a couple of days later when he came back to himself and he was okay.*

Q. *Yes. Dr Horgan was got to see John?*

A. *Sorry?*

Q. *Dr Horgan was got to see John in the police station?*

A. *That's right, it was a lady doctor.*

Q. *And she examined him?*

A. *She did.*

Q. Did you speak to her afterwards?

A. I did.

Q. Did she reassure you?

A. Yes. She told me that he didn't need to be admitted to hospital, he was a bit – he was depressed, he was a bit high and for him to go to his own doctor the following morning.

Q. What I must suggest to you is that the background to your arriving in Abbeylara after 11:00 p.m. on 19 April included that sequence of events and I must put it to you that in fact you had a concern going to Abbeylara that John was a danger to himself and was suicidal?

A. I never had any concern that he was a danger to himself or suicidal.

Q. I must put it to you that you didn't need to go to your mother to ask her what was John's condition or state, because you already knew that he was very upset about a number of things and I must put it to you that he had been threatening, as you record in that interview with Garda O'Boyle, he had been threatening to end his life?

A. Well, I put it to you he was long enough there in the house. He had time to think and if he wanted to commit suicide, he would have committed suicide, and not have a garda do it.

Q. You see, friends of your mother's who were present on the day when they came to give evidence before the Chairman, gave evidence in terms that they were concerned that John would do harm to himself; don't you know that?

A. I have heard that in evidence since but maybe they didn't know him as well as I knew him.

Q. Is that your position, that you knew him so well that you were sure he wouldn't kill himself?

A. That's right, I grew up with him. Sure, there was only a year and two months between us and I knew about his depression and I knew how he coped with it.

Q. How can you possibly give that evidence to the Chairman in light of the matter I have just gone through, the history of your contact with Garda O'Boyle and the arrest of John in Galway on the basis of your worry that he was suicidal and that you would find him in the river?

A. If he was suicidal, he had every opportunity to do it. He had depression from 1992, which is ten years. If he was suicidal, he would have done it.

It didn't seem to matter how many times I denied the accusation, it kept being thrown back at me. But no matter how the evidence looked, I knew that John had never wanted to end his life, and I will go to my grave with this belief.

Another issue examined by Mr Rogers was why I had not gone to my mother immediately when I reached Abbeylara on Wednesday night. To me there was a simple explanation. It was 11:00 p.m. when we finally reached the village and my mother was two miles away in her niece's house being comforted by her relations. At that stage, John had been ill and alone in the house for about six hours. I believed it was essential to be on the scene so that I could speak to him as soon as possible. Yet it seemed as if my decision to stay in the immediate vicinity made me guilty of some unforgivable oversight. It was amazing how decisions made in the throes of our unfolding tragedy were constantly being reflected back at me in the form of accusations.

I was also questioned closely about Holy Thursday and the information Rose had given me about her last encounter with John.

Q. Did you see your mother in the morning?
A. I did.
Q. What did she explain to you about John?

A. She wasn't really talking that much, she was really upset.

Q. Did she explain to you anything about John?

A. Not really, I don't remember her explaining anything. I don't recall, she could have said something, I don't know. Everybody was upset in the house and she wasn't talking that much.

Q. Did she explain what it was about?

A. I don't recall her explaining.

Q. Did you ask her what it was about?

A. I can't remember.

Q. Ms Carthy, this would have been the most important question to ask your mother who had been put out of her home by her son, who was now holed up—

A. She wasn't put out of the home.

Q. He asked her to go up to Walsh's and she was afraid for his own safety on her own say-so. Are you telling the Chairman you didn't ask her what it was about?

A. I am not telling you, I just can't remember.

What I did remember was my mother's grief-stricken face, her shoulders bowed with the weight of her anguish. I could barely contain my anger as Mr Rogers harshly insisted that it was unbelievable not to have demanded explanations from her. She had phoned the guards, little realising the catastrophic consequences of her decision and, knowing this, she was unable to talk to us about John without crying. Pressuring her for detailed information was impossible and, under the circumstances, unnecessarily cruel. Every effort was made to keep her calm, and Trisha kept the television and radio off to protect her from the sensational reporting being relayed from Abbeylara. My cousins came and went, bringing what news they could from the village. Apart from what Rose had told them the previous day, they were no wiser than I was as to the reasons why John had

164

acted so recklessly. Not that the reason mattered by that stage; John's situation had gone far beyond reasons or motives. We knew he was seriously ill and desperately in need of specialised medical attention.

On that Wednesday afternoon, in the last conversation I would ever have with John, he joked about drinking a bottle of whiskey he claimed to have in the house. Alcohol was never kept at home and I'd suspected he was teasing me, knowing how annoyed I'd be if he threatened to mix his medication with spirits. The following day, as I waited for permission to speak to him, I considered the thought that his sudden mood change was due to alcohol, but dismissed it. This was confirmed later when his preliminary blood screen from Beaumont Hospital gave a positive result for tricyclic antidepressant drugs but was negative for alcohol or barbiturates.

However, it was inevitable that the drink allegation against me would come up in cross-examination. I'd always suspected that it was a calculated lie invented to damage my credibility. During my cross-examination by Mr McGuinness, I braced myself for the questions, knowing it was important for the gardaí to substantiate the claim they'd made in the Culligan Report.

> Q. *Would it be fair to say that you were probably in a state of some anxiety and shock and worry when you arrived at the scene?*
> A. *No. I wasn't in shock, I was just worried about John.*
> Q. *In any event, when you did arrive on the scene, is it a fact that during that evening you hadn't consumed any alcohol at all?*
> A. *Before I arrived?*
> Q. *Yes.*
> A. *That's right, I was just after coming from work and my boss dropped me home from work and then the Gardaí collected me and I came straight home.*

Q. So when you first arrived, you had not consumed any alcohol and on the second occasion when you came back, you had in fact consumed some alcohol?

A. The first time when I came to the Abbeylara side and then back around to the Ballywillian side I was dropped back to Devines' house in Abbeylara because I was getting nowhere, I wasn't allowed talk to John so I told the gardaí that I was staying in Devines' house and I would be there if they needed me. So, during the night Mrs Devine made us each a hot whiskey, myself, Martin and Thomas and a few members of her family and I had one hot whiskey that night.

Q. But you would agree with me that there is that difference, as a matter of fact, on the first occasion you hadn't consumed anything and when you came back on the second occasion you had consumed some alcohol?

A. I just had one hot whiskey.

Q. If a garda noticed that there was some alcohol had been consumed, he would be correct in that recognition of that assumption as a matter of fact; isn't that right?

A. I am sure he would have said it to me if he had noticed.

Q. You would agree with me that in fact he would be correct in recognising that fact, isn't that right because it was a fact?

A. Yes, I had one.

Chairman: It could be a fact only if it was relevant and that is that the garda took the view that Ms Carthy wasn't in a fit state to contact her brother. The fact she had a drink is not relevant at all.

Mr McGuinness: No, it is not. As I understand from Garda Campbell's evidence and we will hear from the other members, but the way he put it was that you were anxious, agitated, upset and you appeared to have had some drink

taken. Would you agree with that description, that you
were anxious and upset?
A. I was worried and it would be expected I would be upset
and I had one hot whiskey, but one hot whiskey wasn't
going to make me drunk and I am sure it wouldn't make
anyone drunk.
Chairman: Did it have any effect on you and your capacity
to understand what was going on?
A. None whatsoever.
Mr McGuinness: Were you swaying slightly perhaps?
A. Definitely not, I had just had one hot whiskey. So had
Thomas and so had Martin Shelly and still Martin Shelly
was allowed down to talk to John after one hot whiskey,
the same amount as me.

Mr McGuinness and Mr Rogers questioned me closely about the high
number of phone calls John made to my mobile in the week leading
up to his death. Some of his calls were made in rapid succession, some
lasting only a few seconds, which would not even have allowed time
for the message on my answering machine to run its course before he
hung up and tried again. A list of our calls was displayed on a screen
for us to check and, as the questioning continued, my head began to
reel from the effort of remembering conversations I'd had with John
three years previously. This extract of the cross-examination was
conducted by Mr Rogers.

Q. The records appear to show that in fact he got through
to your number on a number of occasions?
A. That's right.
Q. There is no doubt about that, he actually got through to
your number, so he either spoke to you or he got through to
your message minder, is that right?

A. Yeah, he would have spoke to me when he got through because he would have never left a message.

Q. I am going to ask you something about that later. On the occasions on that weekend I am talking about, I think it is Saturday, 15th; did you speak to John and did you detect that he was elated?

A. No, he was fine.

Q. I see. Why was he ringing you so much?

A. Obviously if you ring someone, you don't get them, you obviously ring them back because he wanted to talk to me.

Q. We know that – do you wish me to go through all of the records of the times he rang you, say, on the 15th, the Saturday?

A. It is up to yourself.

Q. Do you know what he wanted you for on those occasions?

A. He just wanted to talk to me because he rang me every day to talk to me anyway and he would often ring twice a day.

Q. Just looking at Saturday, 15th, if we could have page 134, please, of Book 2, Volume 2. Do you see where the 15th begins there, Ms Carthy, it is about one-third of the way up from the bottom?

A. Yes.

Q. Do you see that?

A. Yes.

Q. If one goes across from the first entry from 15th, we have a call of four seconds, do you see that?

A. That's right.

Q. At 8:36, do you see that?

A. Yes.

Q. That is to your number, isn't that right?

A. Yes.

Q. That was in the morning. Were you working that Saturday morning?

A. No.

Q. What are you saying occurred when that call was made?

A. The phone was probably turned off because I was in bed, I was after working all week and it was 8:45 almost, well, 8:35 in the morning.

Q. If we look at it again, there is another call then at 8:43, isn't that right?

A. Yes.

Q. About seven minutes later and there appears to be one in between actually at 8:35 or just before 8:35 and it was recorded later on the sheet, do you see that?

A. 8:35?

Q. Yes?

A. That is not my number, is it?

Q. If you just look at it for a moment, I just want to put to you something about that number. That number reads 087 73798 – is it, what is it?

A. 9868.

Q. 9868. Is the latter part of that, the 379868 your number?

A. Yes.

Q. Isn't it the case that the 7 is the digit that is inserted if a caller wants to go directly through to message minder?

A. No, that is a 5.

Q. Sorry?

A. It is a 5.

Q. I have to actually suggest to you that it is a 7 that was put in and that in fact what John was doing was calling directly to your message minder?

A. I was under the impression that if you ring and try and get into a person's message, you dial 0875.

Q. I have to put it to you that in fact what you do is, after the digits 087, let us say, the next digit is 6, you increase that to 7 and that will put you through to the message minder?

A. Are you sure about that?

Q. I am so sure that I am putting it to you.

A. I am so sure that I have done it, putting a 5 in front of it.

Q. You see, if one looks at these records, what I am suggesting is logically correct, because John would appear to have done that a number of times, is that correct?

A. Can you try it and see if it works?

Q. Sorry?

A. Can you try it and see if it works?

Q. I think the process here is that I am supposed to ask the questions and what I want to suggest to you is that these records show that John was ringing you and your message minder repeatedly that day. Can you tell the Chairman at what point in the day did you become aware that John Carthy was ringing you?

A. Whatever time I answered the phone and was talking to him.

I never ignored John's calls, but he had obviously rung at times when I was at work, or at night when my phone was switched off. As questions continued in this vein, I felt as if I was being accused of ignoring his messages because I knew he was ill and I didn't want to have to deal with the consequences. This inference was absolutely untrue. John never left messages on my answering machine, and when we did speak, he never told me about his efforts to reach me. If he was becoming elated, such impatience and demands for instantaneous responses to things would be typical symptoms. I knew he was anxious to see Dr Shanley, but he seemed to be holding himself together, and I never noticed any obvious signs that he was elated when we spoke.

Both Kevin Ireland and Kieran Lennon reported the same deceptive calmness when they spoke to him on Holy Thursday afternoon.

As the questions continued and I tried to defend myself, I longed for the chance to take back time and respond now to even one of those lonely, unanswered calls.

On many occasions during his cross-examination, John Rogers pointed his finger at me. The more I refused to bend to his will, the more aggressive he seemed to become. I had to keep reminding myself that I had done nothing wrong. I was not a criminal, even if at times I felt as if I was being treated like one. All I had ever wanted to do was find out why John's situation had spiralled out of control so quickly, but in asking these questions, I had dared to challenge the authority of the gardaí and now, it seemed, I must pay the price.

When he questioned me about my journey to Abbeylara and my conflict with the guards on duty, I felt the familiar sense of injustice resurfacing.

> *Q. Did you think it would be a good idea for you to go down and stand in front of the house when John was firing shots in the way he was?*
> *A. All I wanted to do was go down and talk to him, I never asked to go into the house. I don't think it was a good idea for unarmed gardaí to be there either if I couldn't even go down, and why could Martin Shelly get talking to him as well?*
> *Q. Isn't it the point that anything that was to be done in terms of you speaking to John or Martin speaking to John would have been to be done in a controlled and organised way?*
> *A. It would have been. But if it was safe for unarmed gardaí to be there, surely it would be safe for his own sister to be there.*

Q. *Where are you saying you saw the unarmed gardaí?*

A. *They were around the house. Even when he came out, they all ran because they were unarmed. Why did they run and scatter, and why was it not safe for me to go down to him, a member of his own family, the person closest to him?*

Q. *I see. You feel that when you arrived that night you should have been admitted to see John straight away?*

A. *No, I am not saying straight away, obviously they had to organise things. They knew I was coming up, they knew two hours previous, surely they could have arranged something then.*

Q. *Absolutely, they facilitated getting you there?*

A. *They brought me there for nothing.*

Q. *I see. They brought you there for nothing?*

A. *What was the point of bringing me there if they didn't even let me talk to him?*

Q. *Didn't they get information from you?*

A. *Yes, they could have got that over the phone.*

Q. *I see. And you didn't give them information which you could have given them; isn't that correct?*

A. *I did, I gave them all the information they needed.*

Q. *No you didn't, Ms Carthy.*

A. *I did.*

Chairman: *Was she asked the obvious question 'Which doctor is looking after your brother?' Are you suggesting that question was put to this lady?*

Mr Rogers: *No, I am not.*

Chairman: *Should it have been?*

Mr Rogers: *In fact I am not the witness here, Chairman.*

Chairman: *That is the essence of it, isn't it?*

Mr Rogers: *No it's not, Mr Chairman, and I will address you on that in submissions.*

Chairman: Very good.

Q. Ms Carthy, you left the scene at that time to go into Abbeylara; isn't that correct?

A. Yes, because I wasn't allowed talk to John.

Q. Later in the morning, at about 1:50 a.m., the gardaí went around to get Mr Shelly; isn't that correct?

A. Yes, not me, because they had no notion of ever letting me talk to him.

Q. I see. You have that fixed in your mind, have you, Ms Carthy?

A. Well, it is quite obvious, that is what happened, and that is the way it is.

Q. Well, how do you reconcile that with the fact that on the very next day they were about to bring you down to him?

A. No, they weren't. They gave me a telephone to ring him. A telephone of one of the members of the ERU.

Q. You wouldn't credit that they might have been concerned about your safety?

A. They should have been more concerned about their own safety if they were there unarmed. I was quite safe going down there if there were so many unarmed gardaí down there. Martin Shelly was quite safe, Thomas Walsh was quite safe and other friends.

Q. Well, we're not talking – you're talking about two different places now, Ms Carthy. Where you saw Mr Shelly, the Superintendent, that was some distance away from where you would have been talking to John from; is that correct?

A. It was a mobile phone I was going to be talking to him on.

Q. Had you tried to get through to him on a mobile phone?

A. Yes, one of the ERU members' phone and I still don't

173

know whether he knew I was trying to call him or not.

Q. Didn't you try to get through to him on your own phone?

A. Yeah, but the coverage was really bad on my phone, so I couldn't.

Q. But Mr Shelly was brought around, we'll call it the middle of the night, at 1:50 in the morning, to talk to John; isn't that right?

A. Yes.

Q. Did you go around with them?

A. I went as far as I was allowed go.

Q. Exactly. Because somebody took an opinion that it might be safer if you didn't go any further?

A. Why was it OK for Martin Shelly to go down and talk to him?

Q. Ms Carthy, were you not prepared to admit that the gardaí should have some opinion on deciding what was safe on that night when your brother was firing a gun indiscriminately during the night?

A. If it wasn't safe for me, how was it safe for Martin Shelly, Thomas Walsh and other people?

Q. Absolutely, an arrangement was made to bring Martin Shelly down in safe circumstances?

A. What was wrong with bringing me down in safe circumstances?

Q. Because you were insisting on going down and pushing your way down?

A. I wasn't pushing my way down—

Q. And then—

A. Excuse me, let me speak. I wasn't pushing my way down when I came up from Galway the whole way, or the following day.

Q. You had to be restrained because you were pushing your

way; isn't that correct?
A. They pushed me back, yes.
Q. You had to be restrained?
A. I didn't have to be restrained the following day. I was available all day, they didn't let me talk to him all day.

Probably the most difficult moment was when Mr Rogers asked me about the last time I saw John. This was in Galway two weeks before his death. My chest tightened into an anxious knot, and I imagined my thumping heart was audible to the assembled public. I thought, *This is it, this is where I break down and make a scene*, but, surprisingly, I managed to maintain my self-control, fuelled by the toughness of his questions. It was vital I retained the ability to speak coherently so the people attending could appreciate that I was guilty of nothing other than wanting to do what I imagined anyone else in the tribunal rooms would have done under the same circumstances – reach out to my brother and help him in any way I could. So I focused on John's memory and continued to answer Mr Rogers' questions as clearly as possible.

Q. You see, one can understand your upset and perhaps bitterness about not being able to talk to John, but somebody had to be sure, do you understand this, somebody had to be sure it was safe for you to go there. Do you understand that?
A. I do, but how was it safe for everybody else?
Q. It was safe for others because it had been indicated by John that he wanted them there, do you understand that?
A. Yeah.
Q. You see, it could be that – and I don't mean in any sense to reflect on you – but it could be that John harboured some hurt because of things in the past, could that be so?

A. But then why did he try to ring me then, if he didn't want to see me.

Q. We know, for instance, that in Mr Walsh's case, he harboured the hurt, he said, because Mr Walsh hadn't attended him when he was in Loman's, isn't that right?

A. I have heard that in evidence.

Q. We know that John had said in relation to yourself, that he wouldn't forgive you for having him arrested in Galway, is that not right?

A. I have already told you that he had forgiven me and he thanked me for doing it in the end.

Q. Yes, I heard that.

A. Yes.

By the time his cross-examination ended, I was raw and hurting. The implication that John wouldn't have wanted to speak to me stung deeply. No attention had been paid to the fact that John had tried to ring my mobile phone on that fateful Holy Thursday afternoon. I hadn't received this important information from the gardaí until six weeks after his death and it was included in the Culligan Report. I still can't think about his last phone call to me without becoming distressed and wondering what could have happened if only there had been better network coverage. I'd taken tremendous comfort from the knowledge that John had tried to contact me during his ordeal, but during my cross-examinations by the garda legal teams, scant attention, if any, was paid to this fact. Instead, the emphasis was on trying to establish that John had no interest in talking to me and, for this reason, had reacted in a hostile manner when informed that I was waiting with Dr Shanley to make contact. By that stage, my brother had been alone in his house for twenty-five hours, surrounded and confronted by a massive police presence. He was obviously traumatised and frightened, as well as seriously ill. How could anyone make an objective judgement on his behaviour at that point in time?

My own senior counsel, Mr Gageby, followed Mr Rogers' cross-examination and dealt with the 'suicide-by-cop' theory.

Q. As I understand it, Ms Carthy, on day 23 or 24 of this tribunal, it was suggested essentially, to the gardaí who were involved in this, that your brother made a deliberate decision to kill himself by walking out in front of Mr Rogers' heavily armed clients, that is, as I understand it on the table, what the case has been made?
A. That is what they said, yes.
Q. That has been referred to in the vernacular, common speech, as suicide by cop?
A. That's right.
Q. It would seem that a very large amount of what you have been asked is to try to get you to accept is when John came out of that house, took one bullet or one cartridge out of the gun and walked up the road, he had only one thing in mind, which was that he wanted to be shot dead. That seems to be the case. Strip it away from all the evidence, that is it?
A. That is it, yes.
Q. Knowing what you knew about your brother and his relationship with you and the family, do you believe that he would have decided to have himself shot on a public road, if or when he knew that you were up there and the members of the family in the—?
A. Definitely not. If he wanted to die, he would have done it himself, he wouldn't have wanted some guards doing it.
Q. Had he ever in fact made, to your knowledge, an attempt at suicide?
A. Never.

Q. Had he ever taken an overdose of tablets?
A. Never.
Q. Put a rope on a beam or stuck a gun in his mouth?
A. Never.
Q. It has also been suggested that this was part of a grand plan by John and that it was a grand plan which was in his mind for a long time, that is a clear suggestion being made?
A. Yeah.
Q. Learning, as you did a long time afterwards, that John, during the time he was holed up was talking to the gardaí about a solicitor, the provision of a solicitor, a consultation with a solicitor, a good solicitor, the best solicitor, a Republican solicitor or even Mick Finucane?
A. That's right, he requested Mr Finucane.
Q. Does that, in your mind, establish that this was all part of a grand plan of suicide?
A. Definitely not.
Q. You are also and you were subsequently made aware of his conversation with Kevin Ireland, isn't that right?
A. Yes.
Q. In which he said that he hadn't the least notion of doing harm to himself?
A. Yes.

At another point in his cross-examination he asked:

Q. . . . could you think of any good reason why none of your family or you would be told that John was in some shape or form talking about a solicitor, can you see any good reason?
A. I don't see any good reason. They should have told us and if they didn't tell us, they should have went ahead and got a solicitor when he requested it.

Q. It has been suggested that there was communication up and down the line, if I can use that expression. How much were you actually told of what was actually happening, what John was doing, what John was saying?

A. I wasn't really told anything that was happening.

Q. Where did you find any of your information from barring whatever Mr Walsh or Pepper?

A. Sorry?

Q. Where did you get your information from as to what was happening down at the scene?

A. I didn't really get any information. I read bits of things on Aertel, that's just about it. There was a lady garda, Mary Mangan, she was very nice the way she came up to see if we were okay but they weren't given any more information either, I don't think.

Q. When did you first know and realise that over the period of the time that John was holed up in the cottage that he was talking about a solicitor, when did you first hear about it?

A. It was after he died.

Finally, it was over. For two days I'd been subjected to the most rigorous cross-examination. I felt verbally battered and bruised, but I had endured one of the worst days at the tribunal and I was still standing.

Chapter Eighteen

It is not credible that Mr O'Flynn, the series producer of Five
Seven Live *from June 1999 and a long-time experienced news
and current-affairs reporter who had spent six hours at the
scene investigating events at Abbeylara, did not learn from any
of the large number of media personnel present or from locals
who he interviewed in connection with his proposed
programme that John Carthy was suffering from depression.
He stated in evidence that he did not know if he knew it that
day at all.*
  – Barr Tribunal report, Chapter 9: The Media

We always had the radio on in our kitchen. John was a keen listener,
sometimes tuning to RTÉ, other times to Shannonside, our local
station. He listened to the radio constantly during the stand-off.
According to those close to the scene, he sometimes turned up the
volume to drown out Sergeant Jackson's voice. Detective Garda Shane
Nolan, who was on the roadway at the boundary between our house
and Farrell's house, heard the radio tuned to RTÉ 1 for the one o'clock
lunchtime news bulletin. John was obviously well aware that his
situation was receiving nationwide coverage, but at least he had the
protection of remaining anonymous. This, however, was to change

dramatically when Niall O'Flynn, the series producer of RTÉ's popular drive-time programme *Five Seven Live*, arrived in Abbeylara on Thursday.

The producer had attended a funeral in Longford the previous evening and had spent the night in Sligo. The following morning, when he was returning to Dublin, he heard a report about Abbeylara on Pat Kenny's programme, which was being presented that day by Rodney Rice. As he was close to Granard, he stopped his car and listened to an interview with the garda press officer, Superintendent Farrelly. He then contacted RTÉ and discussed doing a report on the situation in Abbeylara. It would be presented as a feature on that evening's *Five Seven Live*. RTÉ already had a camera crew in the village, which meant that they could film his report and it could be televised later that night. He joined the group of journalists who were brought to our house to record the ERU operation at close hand. Later, in compiling his report, he recorded some local people's pleas for John to leave the house.

The truth as to whether or not John tuned into *Five Seven Live* can never be established, but if he did, he would have heard the following interview.

> A. Actually John Carthy, he is a really nice bloke. I picked him up a couple of times from Longford, you know, he was hitchhiking a lift and I picked him up.
> Q. He works in Longford, isn't that right?
> A. Yeah, he works in Longford. He is a very, very easygoing lad, he's a smashing person.
> Q. So no doubt you are very surprised to hear about all this?
> A. I am very, very shocked actually, because John, you know, he is so easygoing it is unbelievable, you know.
> Q. Did he have any problems in his life?
> A. No, no, he was always laughing and joking, you know.

Q. What did he do for a living?

A. Well, when I spoke to him, like, I picked him up last week on the way from Longford and he was telling me that he was working on a building site or something, you know. He was up in Mayo, he was going out with a girl in Mayo and he split up from the girl or something, because the girl – he smokes and he has a drink. The girl says if he packed in the drinking and packed in the smoking, they would get back together again.

Q. So is it still on maybe.

A. Yeah, it is still on, but he was going to go back this week actually, he was going to go back up.

Q. If you could talk to John now, have you a message for him?

A. Well, John, John, if I was you, come out. Everybody loves you and everybody is thinking about you and worrying about you, and you are a good friend and you have lots of friends here. So, please, John, please, come out.

From the tone of the interview, it's obvious that the person being interviewed had John's best interests at heart. But apart from the information about John's relationship with his former girlfriend being incorrect, I wondered if the series producer had thought at all about John and what impact this could have on him – or was the adrenaline of gaining a scoop too tempting to resist? No one involved with the media in Abbeylara, including the garda press officer, knew the contents of this vox pop until, by chance, Paul Reynolds, RTÉ's crime reporter, passed the open door of the broadcasting caravan that evening and overheard part of the programme being prepared for transmission. Paul had been at the scene almost from the beginning. In an effort not to further ignite an already tense situation, he'd respected John's anonymity throughout the stand-off. It was almost five o'clock in the evening, a few minutes before the start of *Five Seven Live.* He told Niall O'Flynn that the RTÉ news room was not identifying John by name. The series producer said it was too late to make changes. His broadcast was ready to go ahead.

About two minutes later, Superintendent Farrelly realised that John was about to be named on air. He was very annoyed that his wishes had been ignored, but Niall O'Flynn again claimed there was nothing that could be done at that late stage. An editorial decision had been taken, and the item was ready to roll.

In evidence to the tribunal, Niall O'Flynn said he would not have included intimate details about John's life if he'd known it would add to his difficulties. I find this hard to believe. When he was talking to his colleague before the broadcast started, he told Paul Reynolds that he saw no reason not to disclose John's name as it was already in the public domain, having been printed in some newspapers. It didn't seem to dawn on him that one of the principal reasons for not disclosing John's name was to avoid him hearing it on air and increasing the tension he was under. There was little chance of the daily newspapers being delivered to his door but every chance that he would hear an RTÉ radio transmission. But I don't suppose John's feelings were of that much interest to him. Judge Barr summed up his opinion of this decision to broadcast in these succinct terms.

> *Mr O'Flynn's conduct seems to indicate the likelihood of a desire on his part to steal a march on his news colleagues in RTÉ and the media generally by titillating his* Five Seven Live *audience with some details of John Carthy's recent, unhappy love life and to suggest that a lost intimate relationship might be revived. If that was in his mind then it would explain why he was loath to consult with Superintendent Farrelly, or even his colleague, Paul Reynolds, in sufficient time to restructure the proposed*

broadcast if it had emerged that that should be done. It also explains why in six hours at Abbeylara he appears to have failed to address one of the major issues emerging from the event, i.e., what was the probable cause of John Carthy's irrational violence and behaviour throughout the siege. However, I make no specific finding in that regard.

Surprisingly, Niall O'Flynn also stated that he had no idea John was suffering with depression. Since he'd been in Abbeylara for most of Holy Thursday, it seems extraordinary that such a highly experienced journalist could have overlooked this salient fact.

It was never proven that John heard the broadcast. For his own sake, I hope he didn't have the radio tuned to RTÉ.

One of the photographs taken of our kitchen includes a shot of the radio. This was examined by two experts. Both were satisfied that the station indicator showed that the radio was not tuned within the ambit of RTÉ 1 on either the FM or medium-wave bands. It appeared to be tuned to Shannonside local radio, but as Justice Barr stated, John could have reset the indicator after the relevant part of the *Five Seven Live* broadcast, at about 5:15 p.m. It is an established fact that during the time the programme was on air, he was greatly agitated and violent within the house.

'The end result would appear to be that even if John Carthy heard the *Five Seven Live* broadcast, it would be very difficult indeed to be satisfied as a matter of probability that it significantly influenced his subsequent conduct in leaving the house,' the judge ruled.

We will never know for sure. The only person who can tell us the truth was dead by six o'clock that evening.

Chapter Nineteen

*The former girlfriend of John Carthy, the Abbeylara siege
victim, has given dramatic new evidence to the Barr Tribunal
which gardaí claim could shed new light on his mental state in
the months before his death. The woman, known as [Ms X],
claims that Carthy had a dispute with his family over land and
had as a result a strained relationship with relatives.*
– Sunday Independent, *31 October 2004*

The publicity that began the moment the media got wind of John's
stand-off and arrived in Abbeylara continued at an unrelenting pace
for years afterwards. I was constantly being asked for interviews and
statements. Some journalists published factual reports, others
investigative features, and sometimes downright untruths made their
way onto the front pages. I learned to recognise the serious work of
journalists – even when I might not have agreed with their conclusions
– and quickly discovered that dealing with the media is a complex and
often agonising experience.

The *Longford Leader* had been actively involved in supporting my
call for an inquiry. They ran regular features on the campaign and had
been sympathetic to John's plight, insisting that if it had been left to
the local guards and a low-key approach had been taken, the situation

would have calmed down. My family always appreciated their support, but sometimes it was difficult to deal with what they wrote. On one particular occasion, I opened the paper and read comments that I was supposed to have made about a tragic situation in Lusk, Co. Dublin, where two men had been shot dead after the ERU engaged armed raiders during an attempted robbery at a post office. I was quoted as saying that the ERU had mishandled the situation. I'd made no such comment, nor had I been asked for one. Some people in Abbeylara believed I'd overstepped the mark and told me in no uncertain terms to mind my own business. They disapproved of what I'd supposedly said and warned me to stop making derogatory statements about the gardaí.

Although I appreciated all the support I'd received from the paper, I was very annoyed about this feature. I didn't want to become a mouthpiece every time the ERU carried out its operations and felt only deep sympathy for the families of the deceased men. Eugene McGee was the editor at the time. I'd spoken to him on many occasions and was embarrassed at having to contact him and complain. My partner, Patrick, seeing how I was dithering, took matters into his own hands and contacted the paper. Within ten minutes' Eugene phoned back and apologised for any hurt the report had caused me. The incorrect information was clarified in the following week's edition. It takes a genuine person to admit straight away that they are wrong, and I respected him for doing so.

But I wasn't always so fortunate when dealing with the print media. As I became more familiar with the publicity machine, I quickly realised that some so-called investigative pieces appeared to be the results of selective leaks by unknown sources within the gardaí or with garda connections.

On Sunday, 31 October 2004, Rose came into my bedroom carrying a copy of the *Sunday Independent* which she had bought in the village. As soon as I saw her face, I knew something dreadful had been printed. She was crying when she handed the newspaper to me. The first thing I saw was a photograph of John with one of me beside it. Under a large banner headline, I read 'Dramatic New Evidence in Abbeylara Case.' Underneath was a smaller headline: 'Abbeylara family row over land may have affected siege victim Carthy's state of mind prior to his death.' The by-line read, 'Maeve Sheehan Exclusive.'

The article claimed that John's former girlfriend had told the Barr Tribunal that John and I had been fighting over a plot of land which he owned. This 'dramatic' new evidence, the journalist claimed, 'could shed new light on his mental state in the months before his death.' I couldn't believe what I was reading. I was aware that John had made this claim about owning a plot of land to his former girlfriend, but it was untrue.

The fifteen acres of land mentioned in the feature belonged to Rose, who inherited it after Patsy died. Knowing how much John had loved working on his farm, Patsy would have wanted John to own the land in due course, and as Rose intended leaving it to him in her will, that would eventually have happened. This was common knowledge in our family and was never an issue between us. My life was in Galway. I had no plans to return to Abbeylara, nor would I have had any use for the land. It was there for John to do as he wished with it.

John's former girlfriend's statement to the tribunal simply stated: 'John gave out about his sister, saying his mother wanted him to sign over some of his land that he inherited from his uncle. He was outraged.' She also indicated that this information was given to her at a time when John was showing signs of his illness. I suspect if he was in an elated frame of mind, he may have been boasting about the land in the hope of impressing her.

We had submitted a statement refuting it, along with the relevant documents of ownership, but this was private information. To see it headlined across the Sunday paper was horrific. Shocked and upset, I tried to pull myself together, knowing that the phone would soon start ringing with media enquiries.

Sure enough, thirty minutes later, Ciaran Mullooly, RTÉ's Midland Correspondent, was at the end of the line. Ciaran had been covering the Barr Tribunal and was well aware of all aspects of the proceedings. He'd regularly interviewed me for RTÉ, and I respected his balanced reporting on the investigation, but on that particular morning I was too distressed to speak to him in detail or to make any comment apart from stating that the allegation was untrue. The first thing I needed to do was contact my solicitor, Peter Mullan. Some of my friends who knew the family situation also rang, disbelieving and furious. They were willing to come and keep me company, but the only people I saw that day were Patrick and my cousin Rosaleen. She, too, was deeply upset, unable to believe that such a story could have been printed without checking the facts with our family. Patrick was equally upset and angry on my behalf. He helped Rose and I to get through the day and deal with the numerous phone calls.

The following morning, the same story was repeated in the *Irish Daily Star*. By then my shock was turning to anger. The media was supposed to be an ethical body, reporting factually on events, or at least checking facts before going into print. As far as I could see, they were abusing their power in a shameful way, and I wasn't prepared to put up with it.

Neither was the chairman of the tribunal. Three days later, when we gathered before Justice Barr, we were left in no doubt about his feelings regarding this article. In a preliminary ruling, he gave the facts as to how he believed the story originated. John's former girlfriend had requested that she remain anonymous during the tribunal. She had moved on with her life and didn't want to be dragged back into an episode that had caused her so much unhappiness and unwanted publicity. She had furnished the tribunal with written statements about her relationship with John and was referred throughout the proceedings as Ms X.

On Friday, 29 October, before this article was published, the tribunal had heard applications from Senior Counsels Diarmuid McGuinness and John Rogers, each of them seeking a ruling that she should be required to give oral testimony in public. Justice Barr decided that these applications should be heard in private session. Everyone except solicitors and counsel for the interested parties was excluded. The solicitors were entitled to inform their clients about what had transpired at the hearing, but the information was to go no further. My family's statement outlining the true facts about ownership was known to everyone at that private session, yet whoever released the information supplied by Ms X about the supposed land feud failed to include the information we had submitted.

'It is evident that Ms Sheehan's article is heavily slanted towards the arguments of Mr Rogers on behalf of his clients,' Justice Barr declared (*Barr Tribunal Report*, Appendix 7). 'The general tenor of it strongly suggests the probability that she has been briefed by one of Mr Rogers' clients or someone on their behalf who is privy to information relating to Ms X which has been circulated on behalf of the tribunal to relevant solicitors and regarding what transpired on the hearing of the Ms X application on 29 October.'

He went on to say that Maeve Sheehan had been seriously misled and manipulated:

> *Regarding the motivation for misleading Ms Sheehan and for instigating her article in the* Sunday Independent, *it seems clear that her informer's primary intention was to thwart and circumvent my direction regarding privacy relating to the applications about the evidence of Ms X and, secondly, to promote a contention based on fundamentally incomplete information that there was disharmony in the Carthy family as between mother, son and daughter.*

It turned out that the journalist had been shown the statement made by Ms X and had accepted it on face value. She didn't investigate the matter with the tribunal, my family or our solicitor. My legal team requested that the tribunal investigate the matter and discover the identity of the journalist's informant, but Justice Barr ruled otherwise:

> *I do not intend to waste tribunal time and to incur expense in pursuing the matter any further, bearing in mind that the informer's apparent deception of Ms Sheehan has been exposed as the cheap, dishonest ploy that it is. Those who, it seems, were intended to benefit from it are, I apprehend, greatly embarrassed by the outcome of the dishonest conduct of Ms Sheehan's informer.*

He decided instead that Maeve Sheehan should be obliged to answer a number of questions. Had her source told her that the information about the ownership of the land was incorrect? Had she also been told that relevant land certificates, as well as entries in the land register, established it was Rose's property?

In a letter dated 3 November, solicitors for Independent Newspapers wrote:

> *It is the editorial policy of Independent Newspapers (Ireland) to at all times adhere to honest and accurate reporting in all its publications. It is therefore with regret that our clients, through your Ruling, have now learned that John Carthy was not the legal owner of land; that his mother had told him he would inherit the land and that the tribunal had received evidence from Mrs Carthy and her daughter that there was no dispute with John Carthy in respect of the land.*

In his second ruling, on 19 November 2004, Justice Barr expressed his surprise that the *Sunday Independent* didn't publish in its following issue, or since then, any apology to my family and to the tribunal. Nor did the newspaper correct the fundamental errors in their story. 'This is not what is reasonable to expect from a reputable newspaper,' he declared.

Had the journalist decided to do a follow-up report, she would have seen the deep hurt her feature caused my family. Rose's quiet life, which she had been trying to rebuild, was constantly being invaded, adding insult to injury. Somehow, Rose continued with her usual routine, helped by the support of her relations and neighbours, but it was becoming increasingly difficult for her to deal with the publicity. We tried to protect her as best we could, but this wasn't always possible, given the unexpected nature of much of it.

A small group of close friends gathered their courage and asked me straight to my face if the article was true. Even to answer this question was extremely hard for me. If the accusation was true, it meant my fight to establish an independent hearing lost all credibility. Indirectly, it was being stated in the article that I was the cause of John's mental stress. I didn't know whether or not my friends would believe me and could only repeat the facts. The article was untrue. At least they had confronted me instead of talking behind my back, but if some of my friends were wondering about the truth of this accusation, then what must the general public believe? Why would they doubt it? It was on the front page of the biggest-selling Sunday newspaper in Ireland, which also has online viewers worldwide. This cruel exposure was another blow to my self-esteem. To have it repeated in other newspapers was unendurable.

For months afterwards, I couldn't face going out in public. Yet I was determined to clear my name. Rose and I instigated legal proceedings against Independent Newspapers and the *Daily Star*, which had repeated the story. Eighteen months later, before the case opened – which would have been held with judge and jury – our action was settled out of court. An apology from the newspaper was read out in court:

> *On October 31, 2004, the* Sunday Independent *published an article entitled 'Dramatic new evidence in Abbeylara case' concerning the Barr Tribunal of Enquiry into the Abbeylara siege. The article contained the incorrect allegation that new evidence had been presented to the tribunal to the effect that the deceased, John Carthy, had been in dispute with his sister, Marie Carthy, over land which he had inherited from his relatives and had as a result strained relationship with his relatives.*
>
> *We now accept that such allegations were false and that the Barr Tribunal had previously found in a private hearing that John Carthy had not inherited any land from relatives.*
>
> *The* Sunday Independent *unreservedly withdraws these allegations and apologises to Marie Carthy and Rose Carthy for the hurt and distress these allegations have caused to them and for the damage to their good name and reputation.*

It was also published on the front page of the *Sunday Independent* on 21 May 2006.

The *Daily Star* also made an apology in court. Eighteen months had passed before I was able to clear my name. I wonder if people believe what they've read and what they think about me. But there's nothing I can do about it. I can't spend my life protesting my innocence. I've got to accept that the battle I fought with the gardaí for the establishment of the Barr Tribunal was bound to have its fall-out. Selective leaks, it appears, are a cruel but convenient way of undermining a person's credibility.

Chapter Twenty

As I said, I have tried to explain this as best I can. There was no reason why. I mean I spoke to the man, he was very helpful and he wanted to be helpful. I could say that had I been told I would have known but I didn't ask him and I cannot put the matter any further than that. There was no reason why I didn't do it, we had learned, come a good way at that time, as you said with the communication with Dr Shanley and that. That was done and I presume – I probably did speak to him about that, and that communication had been made at that end, but that is as far as I can put the other issue for you. I am sorry, but I cannot put it any further.
– Superintendent Shelly at the Barr Tribunal

Listening to Superintendent Shelly answering questions made my head spin. I tried as best I could to follow what he was saying, but it wasn't always easy. When he was questioned during his cross-examination as to why he didn't ask Dr Cullen the reason John felt antagonistic towards the guards, he made the above reply.

At break times, I listened to people talking in the hallway. The general consensus was that Superintendent Shelly was a 'hard nut to crack'. I began to hear about his controversial career. It transpired he was an old hand at tribunals, the Barr Tribunal being his third involvement in such state investigations. The others were the Morris Tribunal and what became known as the Kerry Babies Tribunal, which took place in the mid-1980s.

I was very young when the case of the Kerry babies first came to light. Thinking back to that time, I vaguely remembered watching television and seeing a dark curly-haired young woman walking into court. She seemed so small, almost lost among the crowd of people surrounding her. I understood very little about her circumstances, but twenty years later I would discover how she, too, was catapulted into the public eye and subjected to outrageous accusations.

In April 1984, Joanne Hayes gave birth to a baby. The father was a local married man who ended the relationship while she was pregnant. She disguised her pregnancy and gave birth secretly on her family farm. The baby died shortly afterwards, and its remains were buried on the farm. When, by extraordinary coincidence, the body of a newborn infant with stab wounds was found on a beach near Cahirciveen, suspicion was quick to fall on Joanne.

Members of the murder squad, including Joseph Shelly, were sent to Kerry to investigate the case. Within twelve hours, Joanne and members of her family had given signed confessions admitting to the alleged killing of the Cahirciveen baby, and the subsequent cover-up. An open and shut case, it would seem. The following morning, Joanne appeared in court and was charged with murder. Her aunt, brothers and sister were charged with concealing the birth and assisting in disposing of its body. This was the early 1980s, when unmarried mothers still carried the stigma of disapproval and the Catholic Church was in a position of moral authority, as were the gardaí.

However, things became more complicated when Joanne later retracted her confession and admitted that she had given birth at home following her concealed pregnancy. The guards recovered the body of her tiny infant and concluded that she had given birth to twins. Yet when the blood group of the Cahirciveen baby was tested and proved different to Joanne and that of her baby's father, the gardaí, despite this forensic evidence, devised the theory that she had given birth to both babies simultaneously but that the babies had different fathers. This is an extremely rare occurrence and would have meant that Joanne produced two eggs instead of the usual one during her monthly cycle. Both would have been fertilised independently and involved her being impregnated by two different men. The publicity resulting from this theory was enormous. As an unmarried mother, Joanne was fair game for media speculation, gossip and rumour. I imagine the resultant publicity and gossip must have been devastating for her.

The murder squad wanted to pursue the case, but the Director of Public Prosecutions decided it should be dropped. But the story refused to die down. The public wanted to know how her family made identical signed admissions about the murder of the Cahirciveen baby when they had no involvement in it. After an internal garda inquiry, which failed to resolve the differing versions of events, the Government decided to hold a tribunal. This was chaired by Justice Kevin Lynch and was established to investigate why Joanne and her family had made these confessions. One of Joanne's brothers alleged that he had been assaulted during questioning. He named Joseph Shelly, who was then a detective sergeant, as the guard who allegedly assaulted him. This was rejected by Justice Lynch, and the accusation has always been denied by Superintendent Shelly.

During the tribunal, Justice Lynch criticised the guards for indulging in 'unlikely, far-fetched and self-contradictory theories'. Yet the *Lynch Report* rejected claims that a police conspiracy existed. He exonerated the guards yet described their evidence as 'gilding the lily' or undertaking 'the elevation of honest beliefs or suspicions into positive facts'.

Joanne's own efforts to explain her side of the story in a book resulted in a libel action being taken against her and her publisher.

Superintendent Shelly and a number of other guards eventually reached an out-of-court settlement reportedly worth over €127,000. It effectively silenced her. To this day, she has refused to comment on her ordeal.

Despite the fact that the *Lynch Report* exonerated the gardaí, the murder squad was disbanded soon afterwards and a Garda Complaints Commission established. Superintendent Shelly, along with two other colleagues, was assigned to desk duties. In time, he rose up the ranks again and entered my life on the evening of Spy Wednesday when I met him for the first time on my arrival in Abbeylara.

As I listened to him being cross-examined, I couldn't help thinking about Joanne Hayes and what she had gone through. I wondered if she had managed to put all the publicity behind her and get on with living a normal life. Was such a thing possible? Or did such events brand a person for ever?

The Morris Tribunal was running in tandem with Barr. A death was also at the centre of its investigation. When the body of a local cattle dealer, Richie Barron, was discovered on the roadside near his home in Raphoe in October 1996, many locals believed he was the victim of a hit-and-run accident. However, Frank McBrearty, Jr., his cousin, Mark McConnell, and Michael Peoples were arrested on 4 December 1996 on suspicion of murder. This was the beginning of a living nightmare for these families. Mark McConnell's wife, Roisin, and her first cousin, Charlotte Peoples, as well as two of Roisin's sisters and employees of the McBreartys were also arrested as accessories. When Frank McBrearty, Sr. was arrested, he was accused of bribing witnesses.

Today, the death of Richie Barron has been established beyond doubt as the result of a hit-and-run accident. The ordeal suffered by these families is enormous, as was their struggle to prove their innocence. Some senior officers, among them Superintendent Shelly, who was serving in the Donegal region at the time, were unable to produce any notes or diaries they kept during the garda investigation. This omission did not impress Justice Morris. He swept aside the excuses given for the destruction of such important material and called it a scandalous act.

> Regrettably, while the tribunal would have liked to conclude that there was some sense of objectivity or independent-minded investigation going on in the context of the unfortunate death of Mr Barron, there is no evidence to support this. Rather, all of the documents that are available to the tribunal, apart from those deliberately destroyed by Detective Superintendent Joseph Shelly, Chief Super-intendent Denis Fitzpatrick and Detective Superintendent John McGinley, indicate that rumour hardened into supposition from the earliest possible stage (Morris Tribunal report, Chapter 5: The Garda 'Murder' Hunt).

Rumour and supposition . . . shades of the Kerry babies, perhaps. But this time there would be no gilding the lily: 'The directing minds of the investigation were Superintendent Shelly, Superintendent Fitzpatrick, Inspector McGinley and, from February in 1997, Superintendent Lennon,' Justice Morris ruled. 'The main bulk of the responsibility for this extraordinary conduct must rest on their shoulders.'

At the Barr Tribunal, Superintendent Shelly's forceful manner was impressive. During his cross-examination, he denied receiving information from Thomas about our family solicitor. He knew that reports on John's medical history, containing valuable information on the effect his medication might have on him, had been obtained from Dr Cullen during the night shift, but he had made no attempt to read this information. He gave permission to Superintendent Farrelly to bring the media to the scene, despite the fact that John had access to the radio. He stated that he didn't hear it playing, despite evidence from other officers that they could hear music and news reports. He angrily rejected the accusation that he was promoting a positive view of the gardaí by bringing the media close to the scene. Instead, he claimed, the media had been permitted access to 'facilitate them and to ensure in so doing that no media person would act in an unsafe manner in or around the scene'. He was unaware of any plan or tactic should John have emerged from the house in an uncontrolled manner during that time. Superintendent Farrelly admitted that he had had no discussions with him if that situation were to arise. When Noeleen Leddy informed the superintendent of Kevin Ireland's phone call and gave him Kevin's mobile number, no attempt was made to contact Kevin to find out exactly what John had said. Superintendent Shelly received this information at 2:41 p.m. and finally discovered Michael Finucane's number at 5:30 p.m. It took *Prime Time* twenty-five seconds to receive this information from a telephone operator.

I observed this highly experienced police officer who'd had control over my brother's final hours. As I listened to the tough questions being asked in cross-examination and the robust answers he gave, I could only pray that the truth would finally be revealed.

Chapter Twenty-one

The Barr Tribunal, which has been investigating the fatal shooting of John Carthy at Abbeylara in 2000, is expected to hold its final day of public hearings in Dublin today.

The retired High Court judge, Robert Barr, will hear closing submissions from legal representatives for the Garda Emergency Response Unit and the Carthy family.

He is expected to issue his final report on the incident before the end of June next year, three years after the Tribunal was established.

– RTÉ News, 6 December 2004

Finally, the days of cross-examinations, rulings, arguments, tears and bluster came to an end. The results of the tribunal were to be published six months from its conclusion. This didn't happen. News of the report's release was announced on a number of occasions, raising my hopes alongside my anxieties. I'd fought hard, pushed forward on adrenaline. Now I could do nothing except await the results. The prolonged periods spent attending the tribunal meant I'd been out of the workforce. My self-confidence was also badly shaken by all that had occurred. I felt uncomfortable with people, conscious that they were wary of me, unsure what to think about the conflicting stories that had been published about me and my family. I needed some new direction, something that would help me focus on the way forward.

The fact that my life had changed so suddenly through tragedy opened my eyes to the suffering of others. People shared stories with me that were shocking, cruel, unbelievable. I recognised the hurt these people endured, and they recognised mine. We were an almost invisible section of society outwardly living our day-to-day lives. I also heard stories of tremendous courage as families struggled to overcome their tragedies and achieve some kind of normality and serenity.

As I listened to such stories, I was drawn to the idea of becoming a counsellor. Suddenly, it was the right time to make decisions. Instead of waiting for the tribunal results in a limbo of uncertainty, I'd apply for a course in counselling. I knew such a path would be challenging and would force me to confront my own feelings, which I'd tried to contain as much as possible. I also believed it would be good for my self-development.

The NUI Certificate in Counselling Skills has tutors based in centres throughout Ireland. I chose to take my course in Longford and began studying in September 2005. Our class tutor was very helpful, and I got on well with the other students. They, too, had life experiences to tackle and resolve. We had practice sessions of counselling and formed a strong bond of trust in each other. Being able to examine myself in this supportive environment helped me identify my emotions and discuss how I felt. At times this was extremely difficult. In the beginning I was quite nervous speaking out in front of the group. When I had spoken in public in the past, my focus was always on John. Although it was intimidating dealing with the media, I was able to issue statements and attend press conferences. I had a cause to fight and knew exactly what I needed to say. Now, suddenly, I had to express my innermost thoughts. It was an emotional experience, especially when I participated in a group project on bereavement. We focused our project on the stages of grief, effects of grief, traumatic grief, post-traumatic stress disorder and the different circumstances surrounding a death and decided to deliver it in the form of a play centred on an Irish wake. I acted the part of a wife whose husband had passed away. As the bereaved wife, I had the chance to express my feelings and emotions to my neighbours and friends, played by the rest of the group, when they called to the wake to offer their condolences. Our play also highlighted the difference in traditional wakes, which people had years ago, and modern-day wakes. Drawing on my own feelings and expressing them verbally was challenging, but I enjoyed being part of the project. The end task was to present it to the general group, who listened to our performance in absolute silence. Grief is such a universal experience, yet we suffer as individuals, and the play helped us share our emotions in a safe and supportive environment.

After completing my first year, I was delighted to receive a first-class-honours counselling certificate in autumn 2006. Overall, the course was tremendously helpful in restoring my confidence, but the tribunal was never far from my mind. In the summer of 2005, I read in the national papers that Superintendent Shelly, still only in his early fifties, was to take early retirement with a retirement bonus and full pension from the Department of Justice. It seemed incredible that someone so central to the events at Abbeylara should be allowed to retire when he was the subject of an investigation by a High Court judge. RTÉ's Ciaran Mullooly drove to Oldcastle, where I was now living, to interview me about this development.

'It doesn't make sense that someone can retire with a pension in these circumstances,' I said. 'It's like giving him a pat on the back and saying well done for all the things he has done wrong and all the mistakes he has made. It's an insult to my family and the McBrearty family in Donegal that he is allowed to retire with a pension.'

I asked the Garda Commissioner to put his application for retirement on hold and recommended that Superintendent Shelly be suspended from the force until the tribunal findings were released. No attention was paid to this request, and he duly retired with his full pension and retirement bonus of over €100,000 intact. Regardless of what the tribunal found, Joseph Shelly would continue to receive his annual pension for the rest of his life.

Then, in December of the same year, we heard that the negotiator, Michael Jackson, was approved and listed by the Garda Commissioner for promotion to the rank of Superintendent. Again, the timing seemed wrong. The report was due out soon. Why not wait for its findings? But our request that it should be postponed was again ignored.

Each time I thought the report's release date was near, I was filled with a hidden excitement while warning myself at the same time not to get my hopes up. With people constantly asking me if I'd heard any news, there was no escaping the subject. As the projected dates came and went, my anxiety grew. I would lie awake at night conjuring all kinds of horrible scenarios in my mind. I worried that something awful would happen to Justice Barr, whom I'd come to respect and admire. I wondered if the gardaí were interfering in some way to block the report. Every time the phone rang, I jumped, expecting news. Taking on the police force was a tough and uncompromising battle. The process had been designed to crack and wear down even the toughest person. I can't count the number of times I believed I couldn't go on any more. Physically, I'd become prone to all kinds of infections and was suffering with kidney and stomach problems. Although numerous tests showed no underlying problems, it was clear that my immune system was weakened from the constant pressure and stress.

One day, I heard on Shannonside that the Barr Report would be out the following day. At first I assumed this was speculation. If it was true, surely someone would have given me advance notice before it was publicly announced. My phone rang an hour later. Paul Daly from DHR Communications, the PR company who would look after my publicity once the report was officially released, was on the line. He, too, had the same news. Officially, it would be the next day. My solicitor, Peter Mullan, also phoned with confirmation. My stomach went into knots as I tried to figure out what the report would reveal. Would we finally get the truth? Would John's name be cleared? Would the lies told about me be put right?

I had my suit ready and my case packed for my trip to Dublin when the phone rang again. This time it was Peter Mullan with the news that, once again, there had been a false alarm. The information given to the Dáil was incorrect. The report was supposed to have been published before the Dáil went into recess, but now, with this extra delay, the government and opposition would be on their summer holidays when it was released. There would be no opportunity for a Dáil debate until a later date.

I needed to do something to help me cope, or it would bring me under. I'd only learned to swim properly a few months previously and enjoyed the release the physical exercise gave me, so I took to swimming regularly. I gave up junk food and stuck to a healthy diet. No late-night eating, no takeaways. Early to bed and early to rise. I began walking as often as I could and regularly used an exercise bike. Like an athlete, I was determined to build up my strength for the road ahead. It was all a far cry from the carefree lifestyle I'd enjoyed in Galway with my friends and colleagues. Indeed, it was becoming increasingly difficult to remember what life was like then. I was consumed by the Barr Tribunal and what the findings would reveal.

After eighteen months had passed since the close of the tribunal, I was unable to control my impatience any longer. I phoned the offices of the Taoiseach Bertie Ahern and the by now Minister for Justice, Michael McDowell, to see if they could help with information. No one could give me a date apart from the vague promise from the office of the Justice Minister that it would be some time in July. Labour Party leader Pat Rabbitte had called many times in the Dáil for its publication. I contacted him to thank him for his interest. He understood my frustration but was no wiser as to its release. Neither was Fine Gael leader Enda Kenny. Having exhausted the government and opposition route, there was nothing I could do except wait with as much calmness as I could muster. I was terrified of being unprepared when the news of its publication hit the headlines and having to give my press conference without having had time to digest the contents. I dreamed of facing the media, my mouth dry as sawdust, unable to utter a word. I was also anxious about Rose, knowing that she was experiencing the same worries.

When I was informed by my solicitor that my family would get a few days' notice beforehand, I was able to relax a little. Late in the afternoon of 13 July 2006, Peter finally rang with the date. This time it was for real. The Barr Report would be released on 20 July 2006. Words can't describe my feelings. Unbelievable relief and anticipation was mixed with dread. I knew in my heart that if Justice Barr and his team had done a thorough investigation on the evidence presented, they would uncover the truth. Yet I'd no idea what to expect.

I now had seven days to prepare myself for what would be one of the most demanding days of those six long years. I wrote a personal appreciation of John and spoke to him, as I often did, when the road ahead seemed too long. I told him I'd loved him at all times, through the good years and the difficult ones when he was coping with his own bleak struggle. The memory of our lives together had helped me not to waver in my determination to restore his reputation. I asked him to help me through the press conference without crying. If I could manage that, the rest would be okay. At night, I used to recite a prayer that a thoughtful friend, June, had given to me. She has great faith in this prayer and insisted that everything would work out well once I had it in my possession, so it too was packed alongside my suit in my suitcase. I needed both heaven and earth to help me through the following day.

I was in Abbeylara with Rose on the evening before the release of the Barr Report. Derek Davis, the RTÉ presenter, rang to see if I'd speak on his show. I told him I'd be reading the report and preparing for my press conference when his programme was broadcast. He said he'd contact me the following day to check, but I knew the time constraints would make it impossible.

When we turned on the RTÉ news at six o'clock the same evening, the focus of the news item was the €18 million cost of the tribunal to the taxpayer for those 208 days of cross-examination and deliberation. It was a high price to pay for the truth, but in the shock that is often expressed over this cost, people seem to forget that you cannot put a cost on human life.

Sleep was impossible that night. I was up and on my way to Dublin by 6:30 the following morning. I met my solicitor and his team in his office at 10:30. Paul Daly and Catherine Heaney from DHR Communications were also present. They gave me excellent advice on how to cope with the media questions that would follow the report's release. I grew calmer as I listened to them. Peter Mullan then went to the Barr Tribunal building to collect the long-delayed, long-awaited Barr Report. He returned twenty minutes later. I was astonished by the size of the report. It totalled 744 pages and felt like a time bomb in my hands. Peter wasted no time in explanations but asked me to go directly to the summary section and read Justice Barr's conclusions.

Chapter Twenty-two

Superintendent Byrne's allegation that Ms Carthy was allegedly drunk when she was brought to the vicinity of the negotiation point with Martin Shelly and Ms Leavey at circa 2:00 a.m. on 20 April was not borne out by the latter witnesses and was strongly denied by Ms Carthy herself. As already stated in Chapter 4, there is uncontroverted evidence that when Ms Carthy was in Devines' house before retiring for the night, Mrs Devine suggested that she (Ms Carthy) and others might have a hot whiskey. She agreed and had one such drink only. This was confirmed by Mr Devine.

– Barr Tribunal report, Chapter 6: The Management of the Incident at Abbeylara – Siege Management Principles

My astonishment grew as I scanned the pages of the Barr Report. One word jumped out at me – 'failure' – and it was used repeatedly to describe how the gardaí managed the stand-off at Abbeylara. Although I'd hoped for answers, this was beyond my wildest imaginings. When I began to shake, I couldn't tell if it was from anger, relief or astonishment. Justice Barr had pulled no punches. In particular, he singled out two specific people for criticism: the day and night scene commanders, Superintendent Shelly and Superintendent Byrne.

He deemed it 'negligent' of Superintendent Shelly not to have personally interviewed Dr Cullen. This should have been done as a matter of urgency as soon as the superintendent arrived in Abbeylara to take over the operation. If he had been unable to do so himself, this task should have been assigned to an experienced senior officer. Failure to do so meant that essential medical information was not available to the ERU negotiator when he arrived at the scene. The report stated:

> Knowing as he did from very early in his involvement as scene commander at Abbeylara that John Carthy suffered from mental illness which had entailed periods of in-patient treatment at a psychiatric hospital, and that Dr Cullen was his long-time general medical practitioner, it ought to have been apparent to Superintendent Shelly that in the interest of devising an appropriate negotiating strategy, urgent medical advice from Dr Cullen and any specialist psychiatrist involved in the case was likely to have been of major importance.

Although the suggestion was strongly denied by Superintendent Shelly during his cross-examination at the tribunal, the chairman again suggested that both commanders were reluctant to engage fully with Dr Cullen in case details of John's wrongful arrest and alleged assault over the goat-mascot incident would then have to be passed on to the ERU negotiator, thus embarrassing the local gardaí. This also deprived Michael Jackson of other important information, including the reasons for John's animosity towards the local gardaí.

> Both scene commanders are discredited by failure to instruct Detective Sergeant Jackson, the ERU negotiator, fully about the goat mascot arrest and detention of Mr Carthy and what followed, and also the taking into

possession and retention of his shotgun by subterfuge
shortly before the mascot arrest and without any evidence
in support of hearsay allegations made against him. John
Carthy's attitude towards the police and the reasons for it
became of major significance in the conduct of Sergeant
Jackson's attempted negotiations with him during the siege
which culminated in his death on 20 April 2000. If the
negotiator had been properly advised as to the cause and
extent of John Carthy's animosity towards and distrust of
the police, it might well have had an important bearing on
his approach to the deceased and how he (Jackson) should
handle the crisis at Abbeylara. He was deprived of
important information by the scene commanders.

Superintendent Shelly was also faulted for not debriefing Kevin
Ireland and finding out exactly what John said in the phone call he
made six hours before his death. Both he and the negotiator learned
about John's telephone conversation 'by way of an inaccurate and
garbled fourth-hand version of it'. Reading the chairman's words, it
seemed as if a fatal game of Chinese whispers had been played along
the line of command and we were left to deal with the consequences.
I remembered how during cross-examination the guards had talked
about the significance they attached to John's comment, 'Watch this
space.' If they were willing to pay so much attention to this comment,
why had John's declaration to Kevin that he had no intention of
shooting anyone not been given the same consideration?

If the scene commander had caused an inquiry to be made
with the Law Society, it would have emerged immediately
whether or not there was a solicitor called 'Finucane'
practising in this state at that time. If there was none, the
next obvious step would have been to ascertain from Mrs

Carthy and/or her daughter, Marie, whether the subject had a local solicitor (which he had) or, if the latter could not be traced, the identity of the family solicitor. Mr Carthy's local attorney, or if necessary the family solicitor, should have been contacted urgently and brought to the scene for attempted negotiation with the subject, preferably by mobile phone, or, if not, by megaphone.

Justice Barr believed that the greatest mistake made by the gardaí at Abbeylara was not preparing for the fact that John could make an uncontrolled exit. His agitation and violent conduct within the house during the late afternoon of Holy Thursday should have warned the scene commander and the ERU tactical commander, Detective Sergeant Russell, that he was nearing the end of his tether. For this reason, the road outside our house should have been cleared of vehicles, including the command jeep, and all personnel, police and civilians not involved in the operation. As I read this section, I vividly remembered the police scattering, the shouts and panic, the suffocating feeling in my chest that something dreadful was about to happen.

Justice Barr stated:

There is no doubt that the scene commander, the tactical commander, the negotiator, the ERU officers and other local gardaí, armed and unarmed, at the scene were taken entirely by surprise when John Carthy suddenly emerged from his house without any prior warning. The consequent confusion and the negligence of those in command led to the tragedy of his death, which would not have happened if the Abbeylara road had been kept clear of vehicles and all personnel, which ought to have been the case.

When John left the house, he walked past the armed ERU officers and didn't engage with them. If the road ahead had been clear, they could have disarmed him from behind. There would have been no need to shoot him. It was as simple and as straightforward as that. But the road had been cluttered with local armed and unarmed uniformed gardaí, and the command vehicle was clearly visible. Superintendent Shelly was held primarily responsible for allowing that situation to develop. As scene commanders, both he and Superintendent Byrne had primary responsibility for the circumstances which led to John's death. Only for the mishandling of the so-called siege, John's life could have been saved. I was overcome with grief as the significance of Justice's Barr's words sank in. My brother did not have to die. I'd always believed in my heart that that was the case, but seeing it written down in black and white, knowing the amount of evidence and the thought process that had led the chairman to this conclusion, made it all the more difficult to bear.

It was shattering to read the following details:

> *Their failure to appreciate the risks involved, not least to the subject himself, if officers are exposed to potential danger underlines the major flaw in the command structure at Abbeylara in having a difficult, dangerous situation commanded by officers with minimal training and no prior experience of what was required of them or of the potential difficulties involved. Unfortunately, they did not receive sufficient guidance in that crucial area from the ERU tactical leader, Sergeant Russell.*

But Justice Barr was also aware of certain difficulties the ERU tactical leader faced when he arrived at the scene:

> *However, in fairness to Sergeant Russell, it must be*

recognised that his superiors put him in a very difficult, if not untenable, situation. It surely must be extremely invidious to find oneself as a junior officer in the position of having to direct senior but inexperienced officers who are scene commanders on how they should do their work and cause them to change structures which they had already put in place at the scene — and all of that happening to the knowledge of local officers and, therefore, adding to the embarrassment of the scene commanders. That situation was liable to be further aggravated by any unhappiness there might be at local level about the introduction of the ERU to the scene and the way that had come about.

Although the command structure was in place when Superintendent Michael Byrne took over as night scene commander, he, too, failed to recognise the risks involved. He was less culpable than Superintendent Shelly, but again, criticism was levelled against him for not personally interviewing Dr Cullen or having this done by an experienced officer. It was finally done at 4:00 a.m., many hours after the stand-off had begun. He was also faulted for his failure to examine John's gun-licence file, which would have given him early information about Dr Shanley. Had the psychiatrist been contacted immediately and brought to Abbeylara, he could have been of valuable assistance to the negotiator.

I apprehend that Dr Shanley would have advised the negotiator about the importance of creating a calming situation to defuse the subject's mania (advice which other medical experts have also confirmed in evidence). To that end he is likely to have proposed that the request for cigarettes should be complied with promptly and with no strings attached. It was patently counter-productive to

211

allow the subject's severe mental state to be aggravated by
nicotine withdrawal.

The contentious issue of cigarettes was again addressed by the chairman: 'Failure to appreciate the importance of calming Mr Carthy by complying with reasonable requests made by him – such as the provision of cigarettes. In that regard, failure to instruct Detective Sergeant Russell to deliver a supply of them at the house when he went there to cut the television cable during the night while Mr Carthy was resting.'

I pictured John being observed as he slept, the rug pulled halfway to his chest, no gun in sight. It was an image I was never able to banish from my mind. The spot where the guard stood when he was cutting the television cable was only an arm's reach away. It would have been a simple gesture to make and could have defused the anger and terror my brother must have been feeling. Instead, a packet of cigarettes had become a carrot-and-stick exercise which had yielded nothing to either side.

My heart beat faster when I saw my name and realised Superintendent Byrne was being faulted in not arranging for me to be interviewed by a competent, experienced officer early on 20 April to assess John's conduct and to check what ideas I might have had to resolve the impasse: 'and also her preparation by the gardaí for contact with her brother as part of the negotiation process should have been put in hand.' At last, someone had listened to my point of view. From the beginning I'd told the guards to back off, to give him space, to stop piling on the pressure. But no one had paid any attention. Who was I to advise the experts? The chairman also believed that an experienced officer with knowledge of what was happening at the scene should have been appointed to my family. Each of us should have been interviewed separately for all relevant background information.

When I read Justice Barr's report on the accusation that I was intoxicated during John's ordeal, I had to fight back tears of relief:

> *There is no evidence that that single drink affected Ms Carthy's sobriety then or later when brought by the police to the scene with Martin Shelly and Ms Leavey. She also denied having had any other alcohol that day. In that regard Mr Devine stated in evidence that when Ms Carthy and Mr Shelly arrived at his house, they 'had definitely no drink' taken. I am satisfied that he was a credible, truthful witness. Superintendent Byrne did not detect any smell of alcohol from Ms Carthy. He was unable to explain why no reference was made in his log to her sobriety or insobriety when brought to the scene circa 2:00 a.m. He conceded that there was no question of insobriety when he met and spoke to her on two other occasions in the course of the previous three hours.*

So there it was – a clear exoneration from an accusation that had haunted me for nearly six years. Even as I read the details, I could hear a radio discussion in the background on the findings, but there was still a lot of reading to do before I could fully absorb the judgment.

On and on the report went – failure . . . failure . . . failure. The same mistakes and lack of initiative repeated along the chain of command, although the decision to call in the ERU – which I and many others had always believed to be an over-the-top reaction – was ruled by Justice Barr to be an appropriate action to take under the circumstances.

Chief Superintendent Patrick Tansey and Assistant Commissioner Tony Hickey were criticised for not making command decisions, despite spending significant time at the scene. They should have ascertained that the negotiator, Sergeant Jackson, had no previous experience of working in a siege situation and arranged for at least one experienced negotiator to work with him.

During the tribunal, Justice Barr had accused the gardaí of being unable to admit they could make mistakes. This was in connection with their failure to locate myself and Pepper in the small hours of Holy Thursday morning. Now he was demanding that they be held accountable for a litany of errors. John had lost his battle with mental illness, and it was evident that the guards had lost their battle for control of the facts as they wished to present them. Justice Barr was demanding that they finally take responsibility for their part in how the stand-off with John was handled and brought to its tragic conclusion. By all accounts, this was a devastating report, which the gardaí could never have anticipated when they challenged and won their case against the Oireachtas sub-committee investigation and called instead for a public inquiry.

An alternative suggestion which could have helped the situation to end peacefully was put forward by the chairman. Assistant Commissioner Hickey should have requested the Director of Public Prosecutions to agree to a postponement of John's arrest pending completion of the in-patient psychiatric treatment offered by Dr Shanley and a report on its outcome. This could have been offered on condition that John left the house without his gun and was brought to hospital immediately. According to evidence from the negotiator, John had believed he was facing ten years in jail. The chairman questioned if it would have been possible to create a 'victory' for John which might encourage him to end his stand-off:

> There is abundant evidence that he was an intelligent man and, notwithstanding the major exacerbation of his mental illness at the time, his capacity for reasoning does not appear to have been seriously impaired. His telephone conversation with Kevin Ireland supports that assessment.

It seems likely he appreciated that he could not maintain his armed defence of the old home indefinitely. It is probable that there would have been strongly in his mind a conviction that he would not surrender to the police, but he had also expressed a fear of long-term imprisonment for what he had done. Bearing all of these factors in mind, was there any possibility of orchestrating an apparent 'success' which he would accept as a justification for bringing the siege to an end without personal humiliation? Such a possibility does not seem to have been addressed by the negotiator or the scene commanders or their superiors.

The procedure of not allowing any concessions without getting something in return was seen as flawed and inappropriate when dealing with someone affected by serious mental trauma, but the chairman accepted that as Sergeant Jackson had no prior experience as a siege negotiator and was not fully briefed about John's illness or his past history with the local gardaí, he was working under difficult conditions. He should have been provided with a collaborator to assist him from among the twenty-seven other experienced police negotiators in service in the jurisdiction at that time. This would have helped him rest more often and plan a meaningful strategy. Sergeant Jackson had been on duty for a total of about twenty hours from the evening of Spy Wednesday up to the time of John's death. This should have been apparent to the scene commanders and their superior officers.

When John left the house, he was shot twice in the legs by the negotiator. If he had fallen at that point, he probably would have survived, but for whatever reason, he found the strength to keep walking. Medical experts were in broad agreement that his highly charged mental state prevented him from reacting as a normal person would to the grievous pain inflicted by his injuries. This delayed response meant that he received two more bullets, fired by Garda McCabe from an Uzi sub-machine gun. Garda McCabe stated in evidence that he saw it as his duty to protect local officers, which, again, came back to one of the primary criticisms in the report – the mistake of having people not involved in the scene standing nearby, thereby endangering their lives or creating a 'blue on blue' accidental shooting:

> *At that point Garda McCabe decided that his duty was to fire at John Carthy in accordance with the instructions and training he had received as an ERU officer, which included a direction that, where possible, the target should be the central body mass or torso of the subject. The first Uzi bullet fired by Garda McCabe struck John Carthy's lower back. The witness stated that it also did not seem to have an effect on him and he was not sure whether the bullet had hit the target. For that reason he then fired a second shot, which struck the subject at a higher point in the back. This caused him to collapse on the road, mortally wounded, and he died almost immediately afterwards.*

The gardaí had always insisted that John walked towards them in either a 'threatening' or 'menacing' manner. The fact that he had deliberately discarded one cartridge could be seen as a warning or a challenge to them to open fire. They had hoped to prove a case of 'suicide by cop', yet Justice Barr had a different perspective. Based on the information given by John to Kevin Ireland, the chairman believed that John did not intend to shoot anyone. His actions in passing the armed officers without threatening them bore this out. Justice Barr asked why, having ignored the ERU officers at the gatepost and the tactical commander standing at the boundary wall, he would then shoot the other officers who were also armed:

Was it not reasonable to take into account that he may have regarded possession of his shotgun armed with one cartridge as being essential for protecting himself from being overpowered by the police and that it was not his intention to use it, at least without provocation. Most unfortunately, Garda McCabe, like all the other officers at the scene, was not aware that a few hours earlier Mr Carthy had informed his friend, Kevin Ireland, in a phone call that he did not intend to shoot anyone. That information, allied to Mr Carthy's conduct in not threatening any of the ERU officers he encountered after he left the house, might well have caused Garda McCabe to reconsider whether the subject did in fact constitute a real threat to the life or safety of anyone.

The visibility of the negotiating position was also criticised as risky and undermined the possibility of successfully negotiating with John. Failure to keep off-duty guards, spectators and vehicles away from the scene and to instruct all officers in range of our house to remain safely under cover at all times was also cited. The command vehicle should have been kept out of sight and a full-time log keeper used to keep track of information obtained and decisions made. Finally, there was trenchant criticism of the failure not to have all the guns and ammunition which local armed gardaí had at the scene collected and examined by ballistics experts. This reminded me of the row that erupted during the tribunal when Justice Barr had mentioned the possibility of the 'fifth bullet' and the resulting drama of John Rogers walking out of the proceedings.

On the question of John's gun and how it had been confiscated in 1998, Justice Barr had this to say:

The gardaí carried out an investigation about the foregoing complaints but failed to establish any evidence in support of them. No formal complaints were made and the gardaí were unable to trace any witness who actually heard John Carthy threaten to use his gun against anyone. It seems likely that if he said any such thing, it was not intended to be taken seriously and was no more than a manifestation of annoyance. There is no doubt that he was upset and distressed by the conduct of Garda Cassidy in taking possession of his shotgun in 1998 for what he later discovered was a spurious reason and it was one of the grounds why he distrusted the Garda Síochána.

He also commented, 'Ultimately, it emerged that the only possible justification for taking the gun was that Mr Carthy had previously suffered from mental illness and that step was taken without seeking any medical information or opinion to justify it.'

The chairman had paid heed to two witnesses who were members of the same gun club as John:

The evidence of Mr Patrick Reilly establishes that the garda recovery of the gun by subterfuge, prior to the investigation of alleged complaints, had a major lingering effect on Mr Carthy. Mr Reilly, a neighbour of the Carthy family who had known the subject all his life, was also a member of the same gun club and had experience of shooting with him. He gave evidence on two matters. First, that John Carthy was a person who was very careful with his firearm and was not one who would take chances with his gun (evidence which was supported by Mr Bernard Brady also).

Sadness as well as anger welled inside me when I read the next section, remembering how distraught John had been over the interrogation he had received at the hands of the local gardaí in Granard when he was accused of burning the goat mascot.

> As demonstrated by the immediate arrest and interrogation of Mr Carthy within six minutes of his arrival at Granard station, there is no doubt that Garda Bruen positively believed that Mr Carthy was guilty of the offence charged and he rejected his emphatic pleas of innocence. It is highly probable that, having recruited Garda McHugh to add further pressure in interrogation, Bruen set about attempting to extort a confession from the detainee. I apprehend that in these circumstances the interrogation would have been robust and that when it failed to achieve its purpose it spilled over into some physical abuse of the accused. When that also failed to achieve a confession of guilt, Garda Bruen realised that he had no evidence to sustain the accusation of crime he had brought against Mr Carthy and shortly afterwards he learned from Garda Martin that Crawford's allegation against the accused was untrue and that there was no justification for his arrest.

Further on, Justice Barr stated:

> The arrest, detention, interrogation and ultimate release of John Carthy on 23 September 1998, including the deceased's allegation of physical assault by his interrogators, was the subject matter of some investigation by Chief Superintendent Culligan's enquiry into events at Abbeylara, including the relationship between John Carthy and the local police. However, the Culligan Report contains no criticism of Garda Bruen or Garda McHugh and is patently sparse on detail. Notwithstanding obvious serious failures by Garda

Bruen in particular, to which I have already referred and which he did not contest in evidence, Superintendent Byrne, who succeeded Superintendent Cullinane on his retirement in August 1999 as area officer at Granard, did not investigate Garda Bruen's performance, nor did he ever interview Dr Cullen about the issue as to whether John Carthy had been subjected to physical abuse while in garda custody under interrogation. It is evident that the history of the subject's arrest and interrogation about alleged responsibility for the burning of the goat mascot was an episode which was seriously embarrassing for the Garda Síochána and not one to which the superintendent would wish to draw attention. Instead, without any further investigation of the matter, Bruen was subsequently promoted to the rank of sergeant.

In all, twenty-three command failures were listed. At times, the words blurred and I had to stop reading. The truth had finally come out. I was holding it in my hands. I felt as if a tremendous weight had lifted from my shoulders. No one could change these findings. Those who had been sceptical, who had offended me and decided that John had got what he deserved, and the mass of doubters who believed I'd never find out the truth, would be able to read and hear the reality of the stand-off at Abbeylara. I rang Rose to see if she was okay. I had to hold back my own tears, afraid that if I started I'd be unable to stop. Rose was weak with relief and an overwhelming sadness.

My phone started ringing. Still numb with shock, I was unable to answer it. It bleeped continually with text messages of good wishes. Almost immediately, my voice mail was full, and I'd no option but to turn off my phone. I had four hours to get through the main points of the report findings before the press conference. My statement needed to be finalised and ready within that time.

The room went quiet as my legal team and the PR representatives, Paul Daly and Catherine Heaney, Patrick and myself sat around the board table in Peter's office. All that could be heard was the turning of pages. We listened to news bulletins on the radio. By now the news was being broadcast from every station in the country. As we were absorbing the enormity of what we were reading, the fire alarm went off. Immediately, everyone had to leave the three-storey building and go outside. I took the report with me. No way was I going to allow it to be reduced to ash! Even outside on the street, people were discussing the findings. Minutes later, we found out it was a false alarm and returned to our work. It was now time to compile our notes and discuss the main points we would like to get across at the press conference, which was arranged for 3:00 p.m.

In Ciaran Mullooly's book, *Death on Holy Thursday*, RTÉ's midland correspondent recounts how Justice Barr held a press conference in Bow Street to explain to the journalists present some of the reasons for the delay in producing the report. I would later discover that my fears about the chairman had been well founded. Justice Barr had been hospitalised during the previous six months. Apart from the threat to his own health, this could also have threatened the outcome of the inquiry. Ciaran asked Justice Barr if there was any one finding of crucial importance in his report that he wanted to highlight.

'The importance of restructuring the command in the Garda Síochána and particularly the Emergency Response Unit in dealing with major catastrophes such as what occurred at Abbeylara,' Justice Barr replied. 'That is probably the most important lesson that I would like to see learned. I have very huge sympathy for the Carthy family and the way they have handled a terrible tragedy in their lives. I think it shouldn't have happened.'

In a statement released shortly after the report was issued, Garda Commissioner Noel Conroy was quick to point out that Justice Barr

221

had three years to consider his report and the gardaí had only twenty-five hours to make decisions. But twenty-five hours should have been long enough to put the fundamental commands listed by Justice Barr into place – mediation rather than confrontation, information from John's family, relevant medical details, a packet of cigarettes, a solicitor and the wisdom to see that there was a seriously ill young man behind his bravado and irrational behaviour.

Chapter Twenty-three

To lose my only brother in such horrific circumstances was
simply heartbreaking. Words cannot describe the unbearable
pain and suffering John's unnecessary death has caused our
family. Life has never been the same for us since John died.
John's death has left a huge emptiness in our lives which shall
remain for ever. For over six years we have sought answers to
bring closure to this harrowing chapter in our lives. We need
answers so that we can try and move on with our own lives.
Perhaps the most important thing is that we need answers so
that this tragedy never happens to another family ever again.
  – Extract from my press statement in the aftermath of the
  Barr Tribunal

Buswells Hotel on Molesworth Street had been chosen as the venue for
the press conference. Our press release was issued to the waiting media
while Peter and I went to a private room to try to relax for a few
minutes before the conference began. At 3 p.m., I took the chair. This
would be the most nerve-wracking and important interview of my life.
Cameras started flashing as soon as I entered the room. Journalists
were seated in rows, waiting for my reaction. A mass of microphones

faced me on the table. Written on a PowerPoint slide shown on a big screen were the words, 'Carthy family reaction to the Barr Report'.

I thought back to the first time I faced the media, less than a week after John died. How innocent I had been at that time, how bewildered and terrified by what the future held. But now, finally, I could face down the wild accusations about myself, my family and my dead brother. I scanned the room, seeking out my partner, Patrick. He smiled over, signalled that everything was going to be okay. He had entered my life when it was too late to know my brother, but I know he would have met with John's approval. I also saw my cousins, Trisha and Rosaleen, sitting among the crowd. This helped me to relax. Journalists were poised with their notebooks, waiting for me to begin. Over the six years, I had become familiar with many of them and learned valuable as well as painful lessons from them. As I started reading from my statement, I felt quite emotional, speaking about John and how his death had affected us.

Finally, I sat back and relaxed. The media attention moved over to Peter, who read the remainder of the press statement on my family's behalf. The cameras continued to flash as the journalists recorded his comments. As arranged through the PR company, they would ask a limited number of questions. I didn't know what they were going to ask, but I felt totally confident to answer anything they threw at me, despite the fact that a cameraman was lying flat on the floor right underneath my face, shooting upwards. But this was not the time for self-consciousness.

When they enquired whether or not my family would take legal action, I told them, 'Today is not the day to answer this question. We have not ruled in or ruled out further legal action. We would have to consider the findings in more detail.'

After the conference ended, we gathered together and tried to settle our thoughts over tea and coffee. Everyone in the room agreed that it had been successful. Thirty minutes later, a number of journalists were still hanging around outside, hoping I had something further to add. I was drained by that stage, and a PR representative told them this would not be possible. My phone was set with a voice-mail message to divert all calls back to the PR company. There would be more journalists waiting in Abbeylara, where RTÉ was doing a live news broadcast. I was unable to deal with any more exposure and decided not to return to the village that evening. To protect her from the media, Rose was again staying on the Coole Road with her niece, Trisha. I knew she was in good hands and, as Patrick drove me from Dublin City to my home in County Meath, I felt the adrenalin draining from my body..

Prime Time spoke about the Barr Report later that night. No doubt they, too, felt vindicated after the in-depth investigations they had carried out. They had asked me if I would participate in the programme, but I wasn't ready to cope with that kind of pressurised live broadcast. I needed time and space to reflect over everything I'd learned from the report.

In an effort to repay a debt of gratitude to our local radio station, the only interview I did by phone the following morning was on Shannonside radio. Joe Finnegan had been a sensitive interviewer in the aftermath of John's death and was fully supportive of our campaign from the beginning. I bought the morning papers in the town and retreated back to the house, unable, as yet, to deal with the public reaction.

On the following Sunday, our parish priest in Abbeylara, Fr Michael Campbell, spoke for the community when he welcomed us to mass and hoped we would have peace after the difficult times we had endured. For the community, this was closure, especially for those who had had to appear as witnesses to the tribunal. The name of Abbeylara has been branded on the public mind, and the aftermath of John's death had been hanging over them for six years. As the mass continued, I thought about all those who had unwittingly been swept up into our tragedy, people like Kevin Ireland, who had become such a crucial witness; Pepper, who had shared my terrifying journey from Galway and remained by my side during those harrowing early days; and my relations, who had comforted Rose when she went to them for advice. I remembered Patricia Leavey, dressed in the light summer clothes she had worn on her flight home from Australia, shivering beside me in the darkness of the Toneymore Road; the Devine family and their kindness on that dreadful night. I thought also about the young woman who had come into my brother's life and made him happy for a brief time before his illness claimed him again. I was relieved that her struggle to remain anonymous had been respected by Justice Barr, despite the strenuous objections from the gardaí's legal team that she give evidence in public about her relationship with John. All the people who had helped me over the years were in my prayers on that Sunday morning. Now they, too, could move on with their lives, knowing they had played their part in establishing the truth.

Over the following days, I used the internet to catch up on the media coverage. RTÉ had given extensive airtime to the report on the day of its release and interviewed a number of people, including Geraldine Clare, a spokesperson from Aware. She welcomed the report, which clarified what Aware had felt were the circumstances behind our tragedy, mainly the lack of communication between the gardaí and John's professional carers.

'The lack of trust in the relationship between John Carthy and the local members of the gardaí, that trust had broken down,' she said. 'There didn't appear to be a conscious effort to make good the relationship.'

In response to a number of people who had phoned RTÉ asking why it was appropriate for someone with manic depression to possess a shotgun, she replied,

I think that view comes from lack of understanding of the

nature of manic depression or bipolar disorder. It's not persistent, it's not ongoing or a constant debilitating condition. People experience it from time to time and have remission from it. In relation to withholding the gun, his doctor had certified him as being well enough to hold that gun, and I think what was significant in relation to the gun was that it was withdrawn from him on false pretences in the first instance and this mitigated again a trusting relationship between him and the gardaí.

She believed that the danger John presented was a perception rather than a reality. He had fired into the air during the stand-off and didn't discharge any shots when he left the house, despite the fact that a number of gardaí were standing in his path. She reminded those who had asked this question that the shots that did the final damage were fired by legal holders of firearms.

On the day after the report was made public, Bertie Ahern publicly apologised to our family, stating that the Barr Report was an important document which the government would study carefully. The Minister for Justice, Michael McDowell, insisted lessons had already been learned from John's tragedy. The gardaí now had protocols in place and would no longer act in the same way in similar circumstances. When Garda Commissioner Noel Conroy had time to reflect on the details contained in the report, the minister said, he would agree with the view that John should not have died and that my family deserved an apology. I was under no illusions that the gardaí would find it easy to make such a concession. The Garda Commissioner had stoutly defended his men and declared that he would not take criticism of the ERU lightly.

However, towards the end of July 2006, a detective arrived unexpectedly at our home with a letter addressed to Rose. I arrived home thirty minutes later to find her reading an apology from Garda Commissioner Noel Conroy.

Dear Mrs Carthy,

I am writing to you on my own behalf as Commissioner of An Garda Síochána and on behalf of all members of An Garda Síochána to express sincere regret at the loss of your son John in Abbeylara on 20 April 2000.

One of the core functions of An Garda Síochána is the preservation of life, a responsibility we take very seriously, and it is therefore most regrettable when we experience an outcome where any life is lost. For the loss of John's life and the circumstances that led to it, I am truly apologetic.

As you are aware, Mr Justice Barr has concluded a very in-depth and detailed review of the events at Abbeylara. He has levelled criticism at a number of people, some of whom are within my organisation, and he has outlined many recommendations that in his expressed view may well have altered the outcome.

I can assure you that each and every recommendation contained in that report is being examined by me and my two Deputy Commissioners, and appropriate changes in our procedures will be brought about to ensure that all recommendations are implemented. Indeed, many changes have already been made arising from lessons learned from the events surrounding John's death.

We cannot change the past but we can endeavour to influence the future and An Garda Síochána, under my control, will do everything possible to ensure that the circumstances that led to the death of John do not arise again.

*Once again, I extend my sympathies to you and your
daughter Marie and I hope through the passage of time your
pain will ease.*

Yours sincerely,
Noel Conroy
Commissioner of An Garda Síochána
27 July 2006

As I read through the contents of this letter, I felt relief for Rose that
an apology from the gardaí had been received, but my anger was
undiminished. For six years we'd hoped for some explanation or
apology, yet nothing had been forthcoming from the gardaí or the
state until Justice Barr's conclusion that John's death was 'a fatality
that should never have been allowed to happen' made such an apology
unavoidable. I thought back to the formalised cruelty of the Culligan
Report; the obstruction of the Oireachtas sub-committee
investigation; the decision to allow Joseph Shelly to retire and
Michael Jackson to be promoted before the findings were published;
and the stress, pressure and media lies we had endured since John's
death, our privacy and our reputations shredded. Years that should
have been carefree had been lost forever. I didn't begrudge them for an
instant. In the end, it was worth it, but nothing, no truths or findings,
would bring John back to us. We would endure his loss for the rest of
our lives.

I was advised by my legal team to take my time making the decision
to instigate a civil action against the gardaí. Would I be able for
another struggle, another battle that could possibly last two years or
more? I sought the advice of my family and friends. Eventually, after a
lot of consideration, my family decided to go ahead and instigate civil
proceedings. I made the announcement on *Prime Time*. As always, the
team were courteous and helpful, but I still found it unnerving to face
the cameras. Growing up in Abbeylara, I could never have imagined

appearing on television or anticipated any reason why it would be necessary. It's just as well the future remains closed to us.

I had hoped to attend the Dáil debate on the findings, but only heard through the media when it was almost over. This was held on 29 November 2006. I tuned in via the internet and heard Michael McDowell's address to the Dáil. He covered four reports into garda activities: the Barr Report; the Ardara, Silver Bullet and Burnfoot modules of the Morris Tribunal; Senior Counsel Mr George Birmingham's Commission of Investigation into the Dean Lyons case; and Messrs Dermot Nally, Joseph Brosnan and Eamon Barnes in relation to the report submitted to the Minister for Foreign Affairs by the Police Ombudsman for Northern Ireland raising concerns about the alleged activity of certain garda officers during 1998.

While I was glad to see the Barr Report get its airing, I was disappointed it had taken almost six months to be debated. Its impact was lost among the other important reports, each deserving of individual attention. The fact that four inquiries into garda activities were taking place over the same period reinforced the need for change within the garda command structures – an issue that was discussed among the rank-and-file gardaí at their annual conference of the Garda Representative Association in 2005. Citing the Morris and Barr Tribunals and the May Day disturbances as examples, they stated that there was a clear lack of management and leadership in An Garda Síochána.

Michael McDowell's address to the Dáil is included at the end of this book, but there is evidence that procedures are now in place. This was borne out in two recent incidents when the gardaí and ERU were called to deal with confrontational situations. In one incident, a man doused himself in petrol and threatened to set himself alight. Within hours, his solicitor arrived on the scene and the stand-off ended peacefully. The second incident, which the ERU handled, resulted in the shooting and injuring of another man. Obviously, there are stark differences between all such incidents, but when I heard about these stand-offs, I felt the familiar horror rushing over me again. It was a relief when they both ended without loss of life.

Justice Barr recommended that the gardaí carry out research into less-than-lethal options for the ERU when dealing with such situations. One suggestion is the Taser gun, which causes the subject to either freeze or fall to the ground. Another is the use of trained firearms-support dogs, which can be used in a 'moving containment' situation. Moving containment allows the person involved in the siege to move within a certain limited area, as John was allowed to do until the fatal shots were fired. If either of these options had been available when he left the house, the end result could have been different. We'll never know for sure, but I'm convinced of one thing: shooting to kill was the option that ended my brother's life and, it has left an indelible stain on the reputation of the gardaí.

Now that the findings from Justice Barr are out in the open, I feel sympathy for the negotiator, Michael Jackson, who, as the chairman stated, faced a unique police crisis. Through lack of management from those in command, he and a fellow colleague were forced to shoot another human being in the back. They have to live with that decision, just as Rose and I will have to come to terms with it.

An important recommendation in the Barr Report is that gardaí should be trained to deal with people suffering from mental illness and that psychologists be made available to help them in situations where a mentally ill person is at the heart of a dangerous incident. I'd like to see these and the other recommendations made by Justice Barr implemented as speedily as possible so that no other family will have to suffer the consequences of losing a loved one under the circumstances that prevailed at Abbeylara.

When Geraldine Clare from Aware spoke on RTÉ about the Barr findings, she stressed the importance that must be placed on mental health care within the community and the vital role that local gardaí play in the affairs of local communities. 'It's not just about the gardaí but about mental health care and housing and joined-up thinking between the various parts of government that have a role to play in looking after those who are vulnerable in society,' she said.

Dr Cullen provided an excellent medical service to John, but where was the aftercare, the back-up, the kind of service that would have helped Rose and I deal with John's episodic illnesses? When he needed help to stabilise him, I was reduced to having him arrested in Galway under an outdated and cumbersome law dating back to 1945. John himself, when he realised that the treatment he was receiving in St Loman's was not helping him, requested that he be referred privately to Dr Shanley and was willing to travel the seventy miles to Dublin in the hope of finding relief.

Funding for mental health continues to slip down the list of health priorities. According to statistics from Amnesty International, mental health receives just 7 per cent of the health budget. This is in comparison to the UK, where it stands at 12 per cent, and that figure is still considered inadequate. It's staggering to realise that in the fifteen- to forty-four-year-old age group, disabilities arising from unipolar depressive disorders in both sexes account for more than the combined disabilities arising from asthma, HIV/AIDS, road-traffic accidents and alcohol/drug-use disorders.

I had believed the Barr Report would release me from the pain of John's death, but despite the many congratulations I received and my personal sense of vindication, I felt adrift in the aftermath, not knowing which way to turn. For six years I'd been driven by only one aim and now, with my goal accomplished, my energy collapsed. This was probably an anticlimax, something that was bound to happen after all the hype and nerves. The fact that my own belief had been articulated through the results of the tribunal, namely, that John should never have died, only added to my distress. My health, both at a physical and an emotional level, remained problematic. I had a number of tests for various ailments, but again, the results yielded nothing fundamental. The flashbacks continue and still do to this day. It was as if my immune system had been affected by the years of campaigning and was still in a process of recovery. But, as the weeks passed, it slowly began to dawn on me that I was in deep mourning for all I had lost. Finally, there was space to grieve in peace and privacy.

Work on this book had started before the Barr Report was released. It was a factual account about what had happened to John. I withheld my own emotions, focusing only on the detail of the stand-off and its consequences. But grief is like a river. It finds its own path and is released in strange and complicated ways. When I returned to this book, I found it easier to describe the effects that this struggle has had on my own life and on Rose. I also began to appreciate the full impact of those six lost years. Most of the time I had been too preoccupied and worried about what was happening in terms of inquiries or media reports to allow myself time to pause and deal with my own feelings. I suspect I was frightened of falling apart if I gave them free reign. Working on the bereavement project had opened a chink in the armour I'd built around myself, and writing my book has helped in a therapeutic way to continue this healing.

I'm now entering that final stage, acceptance. I haven't reached it yet. I don't know if I ever will. Rose is the same. We still protect each other by not delving too deeply into all we've been through, but she also has begun to open up a little bit more since the Barr Report. Holy Thursday is a day to be endured. She lost the three most important men in her life on the day the Last Supper is commemorated – her father, husband and son, a trinity of death that has scarred her so deeply it's impossible to know how she manages.

I lead a quiet life nowadays. No matter how hard I try to shake it off, I'm still acutely conscious of the image the Culligan Report projected: an intoxicated woman creating a drunken scene while her only brother was involved in a traumatic event that ended his life. I find it difficult going out in public and must accept that there are people out there who still carry that picture of me in their minds. In general, the media, both print and broadcast, have been fair to us, but the stand-off at Abbeylara still remains a subject for lurid as well as serious reporting.

The Barr Report aroused strong feelings and differing points of view that need to be aired. I respect the right of people to express their opinions, even if they differ radically from my own. What I don't accept are distorted untruths which damage the reputation of my family and dishonour my brother's memory. Unfortunately, certain newspapers seem to derive satisfaction in presenting the most negative and prejudicial image of John possible. I never know when I will open a paper and see his face looking out at me. Hopefully, one day, he will be allowed to rest in peace. But until then he remains a target for journalists who prefer to sensationalise rather than analyse the life of someone afflicted by a mental disorder.

I hope to resume my counselling course in 2007. I have a choice as to whether I do counselling or clinical psychology. For obvious reasons, both of these areas appeal to me. It will be a continuation of my own personal journey.

Each year, the Abbeylara Handball Club honours John's memory with the John Carthy Memorial Cup. It gives me great pride to present this trophy to the competition winners. The community rallied around my family in our time of need, and I will be everlastingly grateful to them for their compassion. I appreciate that there are certain people within the parish who must have guilty feelings surrounding the mascot incident and the slagging John received about it. Some people genuinely believed he was responsible. Rumour can grow wings, gossip pollute like an oil spill, lies harden into facts if they are repeated often enough. Others in the parish may regret not having a better understanding of the nature of John's illness and giving him a difficult time because of it. Feelings of guilt are common in small country areas when something goes tragically wrong, but country people also pull together to defend their own, and in the main John was treated with kindness and friendship by the majority of our community.

I remain in touch with Pepper and Kevin and speak to them a few times each week. They were delighted with the outcome of the Barr Report, relieved that the truth had finally come out. It was also a great relief to my cousins and my Aunty Nancy, who, sadly, passed away on New Year's Eve. She had been a tremendous support to Rose, who will miss her dearly.

I wrote this book as a tribute to John. I wanted the public to know the boy and the young man who was my brother for twenty-six years. Justice Barr made it possible to bring my story to a conclusion. He searched for John behind the weight of conflicting evidence and gave us back the son and brother we loved. Justice Barr also gave us back our self-respect. For these gifts, I will thank him for the rest of my life.

Afterword by Sean Love

The fatal shooting of John Carthy in April 2000 by the Garda Emergency Response Unit at Abbeylara should not have happened. This is the unambiguous conclusion delivered by the government-appointed Barr Tribunal in its 2006 report of its investigation into John's death. While Marie Carthy and her family always believed this to be the case, their vindication by Justice Barr is unlikely to lessen their grief.

The Barr Tribunal's damning indictment of Garda Síochána systems and management in dealing with mental-health emergencies in the community must galvanise political action. The catalogue of systemic failures identified in the Barr Report, and its conclusion that 'the garda management of the siege at Abbeylara and related matters fell far short of what was required to contend with the situation successfully and to minimise the risk to life', demands urgent attention from government.

Amnesty International has repeatedly raised concerns since 2000, from the human-rights perspective, about the circumstances of John's death and the lack of independent and impartial investigations of all use of lethal force by law-enforcement officers. International treaties to which Ireland has long been a party required the Irish government to provide these systems and, specifically, to uphold the right to life.

While the independent tribunal under Justice Barr was eventually established to review the circumstances of John's killing, the six-year wait for the circumstances of John's death to emerge falls far short of the duty that was incumbent on the Irish government to provide an effective remedy for an alleged violation of the right to life. It is true that we have seen, finally, the welcome establishment of the Garda Ombudsman Commission. However, at the time of writing, this commission is still not operational, and there have been long delays and prevarication in even getting to this stage. The Commission has a very substantial task ahead of it to secure the confidence of the public that it will fulfil its designated role, in particular to promptly and impartially investigate all cases involving death or serious injury at the hands of An Garda Síochána.

The Barr Tribunal found that John 'was probably subjected to physical abuse while under interrogation' when in custody in Granard garda station on 23 September 1998. This is also a serious human-rights issue, and Justice Barr criticises the subsequent garda inquiries into this incident.

Every day, gardaí are confronted with difficult policing situations where mental-health problems are at issue. John's case illustrates the extreme consequences where a police service is ill equipped to deal with mental-health emergencies. Effective measures are essential to ensure no repeat of the circumstances that led to John's death. Justice Barr highlights the need for urgent attention to be given to garda command structures and training, and for effective collaboration and formal liaison systems between the police and mental-health professionals and services.

John Carthy's death highlights the many serious human-rights issues encountered in policing. Gardaí have a responsibility for maintaining public order, but they also have a duty to protect and respect the rights of persons, especially those who are most vulnerable. The systemic and personal failures that led to his death cannot be viewed as historic but as presenting very real continuing challenges to policing in Ireland today.

This book is a chronicle of the nightmare endured by the Carthy family, one that continued for the past six years, through numerous official inquiries. It is a testament to Marie's strength and determination in pursuing her fight for justice, not alone for her beloved brother but also to ensure that no other family ever goes through a similar ordeal.

Sean Love
Executive Director
Amnesty International (Irish Section)

Acknowledgements

On behalf of Rose and myself, I would like to take this opportunity to express our heartfelt thanks to the many people who have supported us through the difficult years since John's death. We owe them a debt of gratitude that can never be repaid, but their kindness will always be deeply appreciated by us.

I want to thank Martin (Pepper) Shelly for accompanying me on that terrifying journey from Salthill to Abbeylara – and for his efforts to reach out to John during the early hours of Holy Thursday morning.

Kevin Ireland – who played such a crucial role in John's final hours. He befriended John in Galway and, like Pepper, has remained a constant friend to my family since then.

Peter O'Reilly and Vincent Quinn – they had the courage to demand answers regarding the circumstances of John's death and to speak out on behalf of the community of Abbeylara.

Anna and Mary Reilly supported us with practical help and advice, especially the decision to contact the Irish Council for Civil Liberties which helped enormously in pushing our campaign forward.

Throughout our childhood, the Walshes have been our extended family, our close neighbours, our friends. My aunt Nancy Walsh's hall door was always open, and she was a tremendous comfort to Rose.

Sadly, Nancy recently passed away. We miss her dearly and will always remember her in our prayers. Grateful thanks to my cousins: Thomas Walsh for his efforts to communicate and comfort John when he had retreated to that bleak place in his mind; Trisha Mahon for looking after Rose in her home during those traumatic twenty-five hours; Ann Walsh who protested about the media presence, knowing how devastating it was for John to hear those hourly broadcasts; Rosaleen Mahon for the comfort she gave me on many occasions, but especially on the day the 'land feud' untruth was printed in the *Sunday Independent*; Maura Flynn, who was unstinting in her encouragement whenever I believed I'd never find answers to the questions I dared to raise. To Jerry Flynn, Christy and Michael Mahon, and to my cousins' children, thanking one and all for being such a tremendous comfort.

To my friends: Siobhan Judge, a special pal who encouraged me to do the tough interviews and believed that writing this book would be a therapeutic experience;. Patricia Leavey, who shared the hours of the stand-off with me and the traumatic days after John's death. To all my other friends, too many to mention, who have been a tremendous help to me, in particular, Regina Brady, Olivia Curley, Patrick and Mary Reilly, Mary Dolan, Chuck and June Owens, Geraldine and Timmy Heaney, Catherine Johnson, James and Aine Walsh.

Also, Jennifer and Jim, two special people who helped me cope with the uphill struggle.

The Devine family, for the kindness and hospitality they always showed to John and I – and for their compassion to me on the night of the stand-off.

To Sean Farrell and Kieran Lennon for their efforts to make contact with John on Holy Thursday.

To the politicians who kept the issue of Abbeylara before the Dáil: Jim Higgins, former Fine Gael Opposition spokesperson for Justice; Joe Higgins, TD, Socialist Party; Pat Rabbitte, Labour Party leader;

Enda Kenny, Fine Gael leader; and Former Taoiseach Albert Reynolds. Also, sincere thanks for the Oireachtas Sub-Committee.

Thank you to Frank Kilbride and the staff of the Park House Hotel in Edgeworthstown for their kindness when I stayed in the hotel after John died.

To Joe Finnegan at Shannonside Radio, for his sensitive reporting and the respect he showed to me each time I was interviewed. To all the staff at Shannonside radio for their help over the past six years. In particular, I'd like to extend grateful thanks to Noeleen Leddy, former journalist with Shannonside, for her prompt reaction in contacting the gardaí when she received details of John's last phone call. Thanks also to Mary Ireland for her efforts to help.

To our parish priest Fr. Michael Campbell for his prayers and his consideration to my family. To the people in Abbeylara parish and surrounding areas for their solidarity and concern. To the many people worldwide who sent cards and letters – and those who called to visit us – thank you for your kindness.

A special thanks to John's friends, his schoolfriends and sporting companions from Abbeylara – and the many friends he made in Longford, Galway, Cavan, Westmeath and Meath.

I'd also like to extend my gratitude to Maura Newman from Abbeylara. She has been a great friend and a constant support to Rose over the past number of years.

Sincere thanks to my legal team, Peter Mullan, Michael Higgins, Patrick Gageby and Paul Greene for their hard work and dedication. Also thanks to the staff at Garrett Sheehan & Co. Solicitors. To Michael Finucane, for his understanding and advice – and for putting me in contact with Peter Mullan. To Frank Gearty, our family solicitor, who helped me in the early months and assisted me through my first press conference. My thanks to solicitor, Noel Sheridan, and Hugh Mohan, Senior Counsel.

To Paul Daly and Catherine Heaney of DHR Communications for their help and advice.

To the Irish Council for Civil Liberties for the many times they highlighted John's death, in particular Donnacha O'Connell, whose expertise was invaluable. I would like to congratulate him on his appointment as Dean of Law at NUI Galway.

To Amnesty International, for all the times they also highlighted John's death – and to Sean Love, Executive Director Amnesty International (Irish Section) for writing the Afterword for my book.

To all the *Prime Time* team, especially Angela Daly and Mike Milotte, for their thorough *Prime Time* investigation also to the people who participated in the making of these programmes. To Mark Little for the courtesy he showed me when I appeared on *Prime Time* and Tara Peterman for organising the delivery of disks of the programmes. To Ciaran Mullooly for his courtesy when interviewing me for RTÉ News.

We appreciate the help and support we received from our local newspapers, the *Longford Leader* and *Longford News*. Special thanks to the editorial teams and their staff.

I'd like to express my gratitude to the photographers and newspapers who obliged me with photographs for my book.

To Justice Barr and his team, for the respect they showed us at all stages of the Tribunal. To Danny, the security man who remained a friendly face among all the stress and pressure of attending the hearings.

To John's medical team, Dr Patrick Cullen, David Shanley and Dr Desmond Bluett, for the care they gave to John throughout his illness.

I wish to express my thanks to Ciara Considine, my publisher at Hodder Headline Ireland, who showed such interest and under-standing from the start – and was a sensitive and encouraging editor throughout. Thanks also to Breda Purdue and all at HHI.

Most of all I would like to thank my co-writer, June Considine, for the invaluable assistance she gave me in writing this book. Her dedication, patience and understanding made it so much easier to tell John's story. I also appreciate the sensitivity and respect she showed to Rose while we were working together on *In Search of John*.

Finally, I want to thank two very special people in my life: Rose, my mother, whom I love dearly. And Patrick, my partner, whose love and loyalty kept me going through the good and the bad days, for his constant encouragement when I believed the way forward was too painful. I'd also like to thank him for his support while I was writing my book.

Appendix 1

Extract from Tánaiste and Minister for Justice, Michael McDowell's address to Dáil Éireann on the day the four reports were aired

These included:
— Mr Justice Frederick Morris on the Ardara, Silver Bullet and Burnfoot modules of his tribunal's work.
— Mr Justice Robert Barr regarding his tribunal's inquiry into the fatal shooting of John Carthy.
— Mr George Birmingham, SC regarding his commission of investigation into the Dean Lyons case.
— Messrs Dermot Nally, Joseph Brosnan and Eamon Barnes in relation to the report submitted to the Minister for Foreign Affairs by the Police Ombudsman for Northern Ireland raising concerns about the alleged activity of certain garda officers during 1998.

GARDA ACCOUNTABILITY
Statements re: the implications for governance, accountability, discipline and training within An Garda Síochána arising from the findings and conclusions contained in a number of reports and the

action taken by the government in response to these matters of serious public concern.

The profoundly disturbing events which are dealt with in the reports we are about to discuss have been, as they must, the subject matter of strong action on the part of the government. The Garda Síochána Act 2005 – the most profound piece of legislation relating to the Garda Síochána in the history of the state – is the vehicle which has been put in place to facilitate change and the inspiration for many of its provisions arise from the fall-out from the events in Donegal.

That Act has become the catalyst for the most fundamental reform and transformation of the force into a modern police service in which we can all take pride. It goes to the very core of policing – recasting in statute from the formal relationship between the executive, the minister, the Oireachtas and An Garda Síochána as well as the force's relationship with local government. It imposes a clear statutory duty on every member of the force, when required to do so by a member of higher rank, to account for his or her action or inaction while on duty. Failure to do so is sufficient to ground disciplinary action which may lead to dismissal. It must be recognised that An Garda Síochána has changed greatly in the intervening years since the events of ten years ago. We are in the midst of a new era of reform that will continue to impact on the way the force conducts its business of serving the community and being responsible to the people.

The government has acted firmly and radically to ensure that the culture and organisation of An Garda Síochána is fully fit for purpose. It is my firm belief that:
— the establishment of the Ombudsman Commission, which is gearing up to commence operations in the new year
— the establishment of the Garda Inspectorate and the appointment of Chief Inspector Kathleen O'Toole and her two fellow inspectors
— the appointment of the four-person civilian expert group,

245

chaired by Senator Maurice Hayes, to advise the Commissioner on the development of management and leadership skills for senior officers, including the promotion of a culture of performance management and accountability, the development of human resource management and succession planning and the development of specialist skills and enhanced training for members and staff of An Garda Síochána

— the establishment of a Garda Reserve
— the establishment of local policing committees
— the creation of a Deputy Garda Commissioner to lead a dedicated change management team
— the enactment of the provisions of the Garda Síochána Act for greater accountability of members of the service
— the new discipline regulations
— the new promotion regulations and
— a whistleblowers' charter
— all signify unprecedented reform and a new era in policing in this country. I am determined to see these measures through and to do my utmost to ensure we never have a repeat of the appalling scenario that arose in the past and had the potential to do lasting damage to the confidence in and trust of the Garda Síochána that all our citizens deserve.

Extract from Tánaiste and Minister for Justice, Michael McDowell's speech on the Barr Report

The Barr Report comprises 744 pages. It represents the fruits of approximately three and a half years of evidence-gathering and analysis, dealing at times with decisions that had to be made in seconds. I have to say that in dealing with its findings I must urge deputies to ensure that its conclusions are contextualised by reference to general circumstances of the so-called Abbeylara siege. The events at Abbeylara in April 2000 were grave and unique in the Irish police experience, were very difficult to contend with and were a very far cry from the crisis situations for which the Emergency Response Unit and the Garda Síochána were trained to contend. These are not my words, but those of Mr Justice Barr. Those words and that context were not well canvassed in public discourse on the matter and did a disservice to many of those who were involved. I think that it is only fair to canvass them now in the context of this debate. It is not our purpose here to second guess Mr Justice Barr's findings or the weight he chose to give to particular evidence and the analysis which led to his conclusions, with some of which I have some difficulty. But whatever one's views on the report, I think no member of this House would wish to understate the difficulties faced by An Garda Síochána in dealing with situations such as these. And while lessons have to be learned and changes have been made, we have to recognise that An Garda Síochána in dealing with people using or threatening to use firearms must not hesitate in taking whatever action is necessary to protect their own lives and those of innocent people.

In short, Mr Justice Barr criticised garda performance in the Abbeylara siege situation, particularly with regard to command structures and training in siege situations where a person armed with a gun may be affected by mental illness. He also identified a need for the availability of additional specialised personnel at the scene of such incidents and asked that consideration be given to the use of non-lethal options. He also favoured consideration of the need for ongoing training for local area superintendents, all garda negotiators and indeed garda recruits. Central to that training should be basic instruction on mental illness and how a person so afflicted should be dealt with.

The Garda Commissioner appointed a high-level group to look into the issues raised by the Barr Report. The group has extracted from the report the matters outlined in the tribunal's report which impact on the policing or operational areas. Each issue identified has been considered and commented upon. Where further action has been identified as being required, recommendations are made on how the group considers the matter may best be progressed.

Since the tragic events of 20 April 2000, very significant developments have taken place within An Garda Síochána in the context of the management of critical events. Most significant of these was the issue of the *On-Scene Commander Manual of Guidance*. I think it is also fair to say that the handling of the similar-type occurrence in recent times by the Garda Síochána has shown that they have learned lessons from Abbeylara and are putting some of those lessons learned into practice.

As many deputies will be aware, I have, in accordance with the provisions of the Garda Síochána Act 2005, forwarded a copy of the Report to the Chief Inspector of the Garda Inspectorate so that garda procedures and practices for dealing with incidents of the type which unfolded at Abbeylara might be reviewed. I understand from the Garda Inspectorate that work on a report in this regard is well-advanced.

Finally, Chapter 13 of the Report deals with 'gun licensing law and related matters' and suggests consideration of proposed improvements to our laws in this country. I am pleased to say that the Criminal Justice Act 2006, which was signed into law on 16 July 2006, provides for significant amendments to the Firearms Acts 1925–2000. The vast majority of the recommendations proposed in relation to gun-licensing have now been legislated for in the Criminal Justice Act 2006. Certain provisions of the Act require a Ministerial Order before commencement. For example, my department and An Garda Síochána are working together in the drawing up of new application forms for firearm certificates and authorisations, as well as appropriate guidelines. It is anticipated that all provisions will be commenced by mid-2007.

Further extract . . .

General Themes

It is my firm view that the three Morris Reports, the Barr Report and the Birmingham Report demand an analysis that transcends their own individual circumstances if we are to get full value from them. It requires us to move from the particular to the more general to distil the various criticisms into manageable and coherent themes. In other words, what do they tell us about police performance in general? I believe that they tell us quite a lot about what is wrong and about what needs to be done to if the performance of the force is to be improved in a way that is needed.

Themes Emerging from All Reports: Leadership

I think it is fair to say that there is one theme in particular that is a feature of three of the four reports, the Nally Report being the exception. That is the weakness of management at senior level in the Garda Síochána in not giving full leadership and actively managing in a way that utilises the resources available to the Garda Síochána to best advantage. It is a recurring theme in the Morris Reports that there is a need to ensure that management of the force is modernised and revamped in line with best practice internationally. The Barr Report identifies similar failures, albeit in a more specific way. It highlights the absence of a structured mechanism for managing scenes like Abbeylara, although of course it states that the performance of particular officers must be considered in the light of what Mr Justice Barr describes as 'inhibiting factors'. The main 'inhibiting factor' is the lack of specific training for those who had leadership roles in Abbeylara and an absence of knowledge on their part in dealing with violent conduct motivated by mental illness.